Quality is Free

Quality is Free

HOW ENGINEERING LEADERS IMPROVE SOFTWARE QUALITY WITHOUT BLOWING THE BUDGET

Stephen Rylander

Author of Patterns of Software Construction

Silverleaf Publishing

The content associated with this book is the sole work and responsibility of the author. Gatekeeper Press had no involvement in the generation of this content.

Quality is Free: How Engineering Leaders Improve Software Quality Without Blowing the Budget

Published by Silverleaf Publishing

Library of Congress Control Number: 2025949464

ISBN (paperback): 9781662970450

eISBN: 9781662970467

Dedication:

To my wife, Alisha, for all her love, guidance, dedication, and support. I continue to be amazed by her drive and resilience.

Thanks to:

My mother, Marion, and my children, Olivia and Harrison.

Contents

Introduction

On January 5, 2024, while flying twenty thousand feet above ground, the door plug on a Boeing 737 Max 9 blew out the side of Alaska Airlines flight 1282 from Portland, Oregon, to Ontario, California, causing an immediate uncontrollable decompression. Passengers who were casually flying out of Portland that day now fought the suction and chaos to avoid being violently pulled out of the plane. These passengers, people like you and me, have now suffered an event that will never leave them. The press went nuts. Boeing made excuses. Lawsuits followed and the blame game commenced.

Unfortunately, this wasn't a one-time quality issue—this was a trend. Safety incidents were happening for years leading up to the door plug ejection. The Lion Air Flight 610 of a Boeing Max 8 jet crashed in Indonesia on October of 2018. Soon after this crash, Boeing received even more negative attention for not disclosing changes to the software of their MCAS flight control system. Five months later, Ethiopian Airline Flight 302 crashed, and the FAA grounded all 737 Max Jets.

In July 2024, the US Department of Justice announced Boeing pled guilty to conspiring to defraud the US government by misleading regulators in the approval of pilot-training standards for the Boeing Max Jet.

How did Boeing, a well-respected US aviation innovator and key supplier to national and international airlines as well as the US federal government, produce so many safety issues? It started with a fundamental change in approach and investment from the Boeing corporation in the early 2000s to control costs, increase margins, and generally please shareholders. Part of this was a change of leadership, and therefore direction, moving away from leaders with engineering experience leading the manufacturer. This change shifted the ultimate goal—safety (quality)—down the corporate priority list.

Boeing manufactured their fuselages and equipment themselves until 2003. After that, they spun the manufacturing into a separate, independent entity, Spirit AeroSystems in Kansas—more than a thousand miles away from the engineers in Washington state. Though the location was not new, bifurcating the oversight, leadership, and financials from Boeing to this new entity was a primary cause leading to the overall reduction in quality.

Reporters from *The Wall Street Journal* found Spirit AeroSystems to have a very different manufacturing mindset than what the public expected from the manufacturer of planes tasked with safely moving millions of people across the world daily. Falling into the efficiency myth like Ford and Chrysler in the 1980s, Spirit didn't build a quality culture—they built a "no issues" culture. A former manufacturing supervisor at Spirit told *The Wall Street Journal* that teams were regularly rewarded with pizza parties and other acknowledgments for reporting low defect rates. That same reporting found that a low reporting of defects was not correlated with low defect occurrence, defect regression, or a high-quality and safe product.

Reporting teams from *The Wall Street Journal*, ABC News, NPR, and international organizations like the BBC reported on a unique process they discovered during fuselage manufacturing called *traveled work*. There are dozens of assembly stations set up in the facility, allowing the fuselage to move down the line. When a welder at Station B runs into an issue with a rivet because of a tool defect, he may spend forty minutes waiting for a new tool and run out of time to finish the weld. To avoid slowing the overall production process, the fuselage is moved forward to Station C, and the work of that welder "travels" down the line. However, the weld is logged as not finished, and must be completed at some point. This leaves the team with few optimum options. Option one, another welder at Station C can receive instructions from the previous station and attempt to finish the work. Option two, the welder from Station B walks down to Station C and finishes the work. Or, the third option, the weld is recorded as a defect and is scheduled for "post-production" when the fuselage moves from the aircraft hanger manufacturing facility to the outdoors.

All of these options had problems. Providing instructions to untrained team members increased the likelihood of weld failure when attempting option one. Options two and three, though retaining the subject matter expertise, were often barriered by incorrect tools at the later station or improper scaffolding. Sometimes the defect, here the weld, was physically difficult to access because of the normal completion of other work cycles; e.g., the weld is at layer zero of the onion, and the production team, through the correct processes, adds layers two through ten into the fuselage. Thus, traveled work as a process, without the right guardrails, provided something like a bacteria breeding ground for defects, safety or otherwise.

Even with these quality problems, the door plug ejecting from Flight 1282 was unique because the door plug was of a surprising design, often derided as unprofessional and poorly conceived by professionals in the industry. First, it was not a door. It was a plug for where a door could be placed on some models, all using the same fuselage; meaning on some models it is a door, but on Flight 1282 appeared as a normal window and wall panel. A passenger sitting in the window seat would never know this was a plug for where a door might be, and they would not require that knowledge either. What was surprising about the door plugs design is that it was attached from the outside. It appeared as common sense to aviation experts inspecting the plane's design after the plug ejection that, like a door, it should be larger on the inside than the outside so that it could not eject. Instead, the assemblers follow instructions to mount the door plug from the outside and secure it on the inside with a series of levers and latches. So the failure of these locking mechanisms allowed the plug to escape the plane, whereas a plug slightly larger than its opening, mounted from the inside, would not be able to escape.

Spirit AeroSystems did not build a quality-based culture—they built a "no defects" culture and provided incentives not to report defects. Poor design, a lack of quality control, and an overall absence of responsibility led to lives lost, trauma, and massive amounts of shareholder erosion.

It's a Challenge

If you've picked up this book, you've most likely experienced some type of professional quality issues. For others, reading this book's introduction may be just about curiosity. So let's get honest, since this book is focused on software systems and technology—times are rough, the quality of your systems may look okay, but you know that it's not fine. The product is just skating by, and the experience of shipping software is painful. Competitors are nipping at your heels, or squarely in front, and peers and internal customers complain. Engineering is always to blame, no matter what the circumstance is. You can't drive quality through testing alone; the cycles are overspent, and everyone feels oversubscribed. Quality is slowly sinking, and it's not what anyone intended.

Let's look at an example of why quality appears so hard from the outside—the complexity of financial systems.

First off, financial systems are inherently complex because their subject matter is. They often involve intricate financial calculations and algorithms handlings topics like risk assessment, portfolio valuations, or pricing models. Then, all of this work requires integration with other financial or management systems, modern or legacy. On top of this work are constantly evolving regulatory requirements like SOX, PCI, or GDPR. To meet those requirements the software must create accurate, auditable reporting requiring copious volumes of quality assurance. This is all wrapped with zero tolerance for errors. Errors means that an individual can't pay their mortgage and that IRS submissions are incorrect. In some cases, in the financial markets, an error could mean a massive liability, producing misreporting of public data to the SEC and Wall Street—these problems can result in nonstop lawsuits and governmental fines plus reputational damage accruing by the minute.

The data involved in this type of environment is constantly at risk from cyber criminals, geo-political coercion, and espionage. The data must be kept private from black hats, internal employees, and any unauthorized parties, requiring non-trivial layers of role-based authentication methods. Many of these financial systems are global in nature, requiring quality assurances of everything mentioned above in foreign and multiple marketplaces like the US, UK, EU, Canada, and Asia. Of course, now that these systems are geographically spread out, performance will undoubtedly become an issue and requires management. A slow component can easily become as critical an issue as no data at all.

The scale and scope of these systems is diverse and complex, made of multiple teams, cultures, time zones, and accountability levels. These requirements make testing end-to-end systems a challenge and edge case detection harder than climbing out of a deep hole. Often, well-intentioned teams can't even test appropriately as they don't have access to the restricted data sets, conversely creating synthetic data to test with. Synthetic data is about as good as it sounds—a good stand-in until it's not anymore. (In the early 2000s, aluminum bike frames were replaced with lighter-weight graphite frames for professional races. These bikes were better—until they broke apart without notice.)

The examples above focus on financial systems. You can replace that industry with any of your choice—health care, retail, transportation, media, education—the list goes on.

The Solution

The journey to sustaining quality in software development hinges on the willingness to confront hard truths and adjust practices at every step. By embedding quality checkpoints throughout the process rather than relegating them to the final stages, organizations can avoid crisis-driven fixes and instead foster a culture where excellence is expected, not exceptional. This proactive approach empowers teams to anticipate issues, adapt efficiently, and deliver solutions that stand the test of time, underscoring the profound impact of systematic change on long-term success.

Let's start with a question: What is quality? Quality occurs when a process or product satisfies customers, is fit for its purpose, and generally exceeds expectations with value and reliability. Therefore, low-quality software is missing those attributes.

You may be looking at this book to simply challenge the seemingly absurd title of *Quality Is Free*. Conversely, the reader desires justification for why quality is expensive. But that's not the best way to frame it. *The better question is what makes cheap things cheap.* See, it's easier to point out the problems than the solutions. So let's get those out of the way now.

You've been told a lie. Quality is not expensive.

Almost all the action taken in software development can be modified, without additional cost, to create quality.

Software is stuck.

Technology always progresses. But how we build software, if anything, went backward, and quality is becoming more and more expensive. Why does Amazon need over thirty thousand programmers? Because quality is hard. They make up for quality in volume and fast failures and massive infrastructure investments to shuffle users from old systems to new systems, to servers that work and clouds that fail. It's all ephemeral. There is no Amazon. Is this quality? By obfuscating everything, building in massive redundancy—is that the return?

But, if you're reading this book, you have software. It's not ephemeral—it's quite real, it's right in front of you, and it's expensive.

I have a proposition. *Quality Is Free.* By combining the right set of techniques, avoiding dogma, and not chasing the shiniest ball, you too can attain quality for free.

The current accepted approach to building quality, mission-critical software today is wrong because of its reliance on nonstop capital injections. This book explains why that is and what you can do about it.

There is a better way. Producing higher quality requires a change to inputs. The path is long, but it's also straightforward. Bake quality into your products and systems by adjusting your processes to create the system. This means addressing the entire build cycle through patterns, practices, and mindsets. This book will help you understand the problems scrambling your teams today that you can't clearly see through the opaqueness of building software. As you learn about the things you didn't know you didn't know, the fog dissipates, and making the right decisions on what to do first, second, and next becomes self-evident.

> This book challenges conventional notions around software development practices by presenting a compelling argument for embracing quality as an inherent aspect that can be attained without excessive financial burdens or complexity. It encourages readers to rethink their approach toward building software systems with an emphasis on making informed decisions that prioritize long-term success over short-sighted solutions.
>
> High-quality software systems are possible when you make choices that drop you into that pit of success.

Introducing the Book

Below is an overview of what you will learn throughout the book. These chapters will improve your practice as an individual contributor, developer, tester, manager, or senior leader, exposing strategies and techniques to achieve high-quality results without significant capital increases. Of course, you can feel free to skip to the chapters of most interest, but I recommend reading the book cover to cover as the sequence is purposeful.

1. Understand the pain and problem of quality (Chapter 1)
2. Manage defects during construction (Chapter 2)
3. Dial in your decision-making process (Chapter 3)
4. Simplify as you go (Chapter 4)
5. Avoiding useless trends (Chapter 5)
6. Design each project to win (Chapter 6)
7. Understanding and using control patterns (Chapter 7)
8. Use a software construction system (Chapters 8 & 9)

Background and Origin of the Book

Everyone has an opinion. But not everyone can be right. I've progressed my career listening, learning, and respecting those around me while taking the best practices from the smartest, most successful outcome-focused leaders I had the opportunity to work near. In some cases, they are the experts—I am the receiver and willing party to write the book for others to share their knowledge. I've worked in small and large teams—but most importantly in teams scaling highly critical, secure datasets with deadline-driven SaaS deliveries.

The idea for this book originated shortly after I published my first book, *Patterns of Software Construction*. While the first book came from the desire to help teams from repeating the same problems continuously, this book stemmed from a series of conversations on why some of our software was running into expensive quality problems. My largest software products continued to deliver rave reviews from customers while some of the smaller were struggling. Why? The team's leaders always stated more "investment" into quality assurance was required. I disagreed. The teams were not understaffed at all! Looking under the hood, I rapidly realized these teams couldn't conceptualize defect rates, backlogs, or how to make the right decisions; got caught up with trends; and weren't following decent project construction or the delivery system from our successful product teams. First, I fixed that, then started this book.

What this Book Is and Is Not

This is not an anthology book of chapters written by different people and then edited together, pretending to be one book. It's not full of interviews with leaders and their stream of consciousness. It's not full of technical details on the latest trendiest tool destined to be shelfware while the book becomes a monitor stand or doorstop. I wrote this book to help the reader and bring unique perspectives to industry. With that, it's still just a book and, hopefully, a useful component in your success.

Let's Roll

Thinking more critically about quality is the first step in this journey, and there is a lot of valuable content ahead. I'm glad you're here—let's roll.

Part 1 - Unsticking Software Development

"Quality is the best business plan." - John Lasseter, 2013, Chief Creative Office, Pixar

1 – Thinking About Quality

The update, when executed on Windows hosts, generated the insidious blue screen of death, making computers unusable. This happened on July 19, 2024, when the security company CrowdStrike deployed a software update leading to cascading negative effects across global IT systems. They not only had a bug in their software, but they also had a failure in their testing and patch deployment process.

Microsoft released this statement the next day: "We currently estimate that CrowdStrike's update affected 8.5 million Windows devices, or less than one percent of all Windows machines. While the percentage was small, the broad economic and societal impacts reflect the use of CrowdStrike by enterprises that run many critical services."

That 8.5 million devices proved to be but a subset of the total affected devices.

The failed change brought down airlines' IT systems, stranding travelers, along with bringing some banking systems to a halt. Still the outage continued spreading—crashing local TV, hundreds of hospital systems, and things as simple as checking out books at local libraries. The UK's Sky News went offline along with numerous television channels in France. And these reports don't even account for the millions of frustrated end users around the world.

The economic impact is hard to measure. The disruption and destruction rippled so rapidly and so vastly, measuring it all without copious voluntary reporting is impossible. *The Wall Street Journal* reported Delta Airlines lost $500 million because of the outage, but that is a conservative estimate.

"Between not just the loss of revenue, but the tens of millions of dollars per day in compensation and hotels. We did everything we could to take care of our customers over that time," Delta CEO Ed Bastian said.

If hospitals, schools, and financial markets weren't bad enough, even some of the US's 911 emergency responses systems faced errors.

Medical systems around the world went offline, suffering as CrowdStrike's update glitch brought Windows PCs down on that Friday morning. Bloomberg reported that British hospitals were having trouble pulling up important patient data, while New York's Memorial Sloan Kettering Cancer Center had to delay the start of any surgical procedures that used anesthesia.

It's hard to imagine 8.5 million of anything. But let's try. New York City, as of this writing, has 8.8 million residents. So imagine an electrical blackout for the entire city of New York—like an apocalyptic movie without the zombies or monsters. Just one Friday morning, everything goes offline and dark. Or like a tsunami that crashes on every shoreline in the world, in unison, destroying on the way in and then receding back into the tumultuous depths with all your project deadlines, customers, and revenue.

And, regarding the example of CloudStrike, all this was from a company whose mission is keeping our systems safe—these are the good guys!

CrowdStrike's nuclear blast to the world's IT systems didn't result from their release process, a tooling issue, or a lack of deep technical proficiency. They possessed all those traits in multitudes, attracting talented people to work in ideal, comfortable open office floor plans across more than thirty-two offices worldwide. Capital investment, staff, hardware, and training was never an issue for them. They had all the creature comforts—hybrid work, equitable operational models, team-based planning, and flexible schedules. Few constraints held the company down—and they could be as casual or aggressive as they wanted in some regards.

They caused this problem with the Falcon sensor on Windows, almost solely, because they let quality slip. They failed to properly test boundary conditions, a classic computer science bug, attempting to read twenty-one items from a file that only contained twenty.

We are doing it wrong.

The industry response to increased complexity over the lasty twenty years has become more egalitarian and casual in development practices. There is more experimentation, more loosely typed languages, and loser constraints.

Wait. Does that make sense?

It doesn't make sense.

If you're building marketing websites or fail-fast startup consumer apps, then this chapter may seem obtuse.

Our focus is on software that must work. Software that has a budget to build, maintenance costs, and a chance of failure. Most times it's not okay to extinguish your budget because there is another round of funding coming. This book focuses on mission-critical software that runs the economy—from companies that run businesses with P&Ls, shareholders, capital investment, and traditional profit-based accounting structures.

Rotten Apples and Old Cars

What if something smells like an apple and looks like an apple, but when you bite into it—it's rotten. Is it still an apple? Yes, it's an apple.

But it's useless.

Once CrowdStrike's software became the antithesis of working software, it was a rotten apple. Shiny and appealing from the outside but, inside, starting to rot. It just takes time for that rot to make its way outside.

Some foods look great, and taste great, but will kill you. How many cheeseburgers can someone eat before a cardiologist is required? Just because commercials for burgers and fries sound great, and you are told they're great, doesn't mean they won't kill you in the long run.

The same goes for the marketing hype around much of the software industry and deflecting practices that inherently produce quality versus those that feel comfortable. The enterprise software industry tries hard to convince everyone (you) that your systems are rotten apples, which, magically, only they can fix—with yet more software! These towers of software (stacks) are more like piles of pizza boxes, lazily swaying, eventually falling over in unpredictable ways.

This isn't very different to the systems many of us work on. One decision, then another, then another equals a mountain of decisions either moving us forward or caving to inter-political, socio-technical, or just plain ignorant demands.

Finally, consider a 1995 Toyota 4Runner on blocks. It looks like a 4Runner, it smells like one—but it doesn't drive. Is it useless? No. Beyond the value of the parts and metal, it's fixable. Belts, rods, engines, and tires are all serviceable, like software. With some effort, a few parts, and a little grease, software can be fixed.

Don't confuse a rotten apple for an old car.

Success Makes You Lazy

Teams that win eventually lose, even if they still have the best players. Why? Because the desire is gone—and that unmeasurable quantity is responsible for more backsliding change than we acknowledge.

On August 14, 2024, Eric Schmidt, former Google CEO, said at a Stanford forum that the reason Google is behind in AI (to the market) is because of Google's (post-Schmidt) social well-being policies and work from home setups. He received pressure immediately and asked Stanford to take the video down after around forty thousand views. But the damage was done. The cat was out of the bag. Schmidt said what the New York finance maestros have been saying for years: Prioritizing social policies over business is bad for business. And Google, no matter who's at the wheel, is a for-profit entity owned by shareholders.

Google was behind in AI because they took their eye off the ball and were focused on non-innovation, as clearly stated by Schmidt. If he doesn't have an insight into Google, then who would?

And how did the public even know to criticize the world's most successful software company? Because Google spit out their first Gemini AI engine ejecting false history and super-politicized-to-be-corrected nonsense. See, queries couldn't even make it to Google's early consumer-facing AI chat product—Google engineers built a layer in front of the generative search engine to interpret questions, and this software was riddled with defects and incorrectly trained itself because they weren't focused on quality first (they did eventually fix it all).

They weren't "not focused" on quality; as in, the incredibly smart and talented engineers weren't trying to cause issues. They believed they were amazing, infallible, as the Google Mountainview campus swaddled them in their glowing primary color–hued light and care. So, as Schmidt pointed out honestly, providing some historical context to today's problems, Google staff looked in a different direction, put their focus somewhere else, and let quality slip. Since they were now aiming west, and not toward quality, they couldn't achieve quality.

Why? Because they were aiming elsewhere.

What makes this case special is the scale. Google, like the great and mighty Oz—and now everyone in the world saw behind the curtain—and it's just more people.

Why doesn't this thing work?

What is the ultimate failure in software? Software that isn't even working! Much like the electricity earlier, knowledge workers without software are just expensive seat warmers.

And let's face it; it may not even be the code a team wrote—it's all part of a bigger system of systems. Please see figure 1.1 below, where your software is just a pawn inside many other layers that you have little control over.

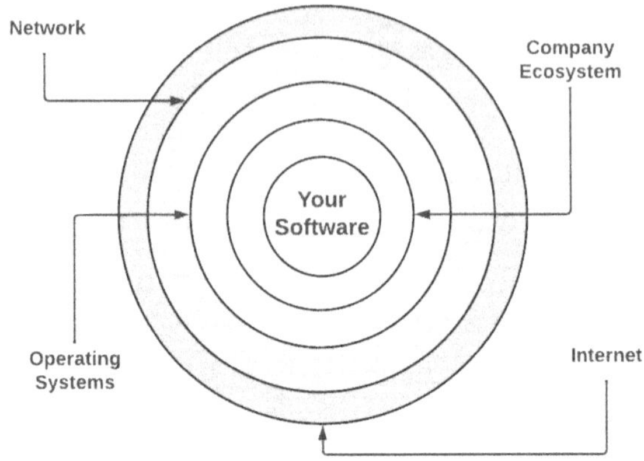

Figure 1.1 - Nested All the Way

Every time a user double-clicks a screen element and nothing happens, we see productivity lost. And those results are staggering.

Low Quality Contributes to Low Economic Productivity

The financial markets (Wall Street) may get hung up on the machinations of the Federal Reserve, trying to predict their next moves like some lost, arcane science, but it's for naught. The metric that isn't as interesting to most is productivity.

For the last two decades, the US economy has lagered with anemic productivity growth, costing households tens of thousands of dollars in income. This wasn't predicated (of course). The internet, the dotcom boom, iPhones, Alexa voice-enabled assistants, generative AI, fiber-to-the-front-door, car Wi-Fi, quad-core chips, and cheap laptops should have "democratized" technology and driven productivity growth through the roof. Yet that didn't happen.

Why?

The technology and software provided to enterprises that drive white-collar, blue-chip growth has failed. The software systems to, say, fly planes have failed. Consultancies that build software for banks, manufacturing, trading, crypto, the public sector, the private sector, sports teams, accounting—they all have massive failures to show.

Software is still the most complex thing mankind makes. And we are generally not good at it.

Wait. Don't big-tech Silicon Valley companies produce high-quality software?

Yes, probably, look at their success. But, what makes you presuppose this? Have you reviewed their defect backlog? Do they have requirements? Or is it just a massively-funded factory of innovation against 1) Meta (anything and everything) or 2) Ecommerce, which is interesting but not complex or regulated.

Really, how can you compare Facebook Marketplace with tens of millions of users (including fake users) to IRS tax-filing software? One has only the boundaries arbitrarily applied to their preference, and the other is either right or wrong. And you can't afford to be wrong working with the revenue systems of the US, software running health care, or banking systems.

Most Software Is Like A Soft Boiled Egg

A lot of today's business software is built by low-cost, globally distributed teams who are told to "just implement the requirements." The worst thing you can do is design and build software to requirements alone—which we'll discuss in Chapter 3.

If you are a practitioner who has painfully written the code behind any serious software solution, you are probably still nodding your head. Much of it misses the mark, and you know it, and your users know it.

The one thing we should not do is pretend that the software failing around us is somehow good. It is wishful thinking to say that "as long as we're agile and delivering value, everything is good." That is how you go out of business, lose critical financial records, blackout a major metropolitan area, or strand hundreds of thousands of people at an airport.

And yes—people lose their jobs over this.

Quality is not just about bugs.

It's about system software design. It's about performance and availability. And more than anything, it's about perception.

There are so many viewpoints on what quality is that it's becoming a self-defeating conversation. Everyone involved, or even in a nearby orbit of a software development project, has an opinion. For instance, someone that works directly with clients may say a missing feature is a lack of quality.

Is that true?

Of course not. The missing feature isn't low quality. It's not even there—so how is it measured as low quality or low value? It's not possible. So let's rule those cases out right away. Quality includes perceptions—but it's not about opinions. We will get more into that below.

"Quality is everyone's responsibility." - **W. Edwards Deming**

Various Views of Quality

Of course, it depends on who's looking. It's the curse of the observer. If you're looking at a bald eagle from underneath, it will look different than if you are looking at it directly. And it will look even more obtuse, or scary, if that eagle is swooping down at you with its talons, thinking you're something to pluck into the air. The lesson: Where you're standing makes all the difference.

You can capture real quality in each of these views using techniques that exist today. You don't need new practice, or to purchase new software, or hire new types of engineers to have fast, available, and timely software. Creating targets in each area and moving toward them systematically achieves results by uncovering quality, not creating it out of nothing.

This is how others look at your systems.

Security

- How likely are we to have a data breach?
- Do we have the right certifications for customers to buy our software?
- Are we going to get hacked and lose it all?

Customer Quality Metrics

Customer metrics are varied and subjective—because like so many things in this non-regulated industry, there is no general agreement.

- User Satisfaction
- Net Promoter Score
- Customer and User Surveys
- Customer Retention Rates

Fast

Like all modern things, the expectation is fast, fast, fast for all software systems. The expectation is fast even for software that has no such requirement—like, say, crunching a single mortgage application. The difference of half a second and five seconds provides close to zero business differentiation, yet the expectation is that operation performs like a Google search for "coffee near me."

There is no other feature that is viewed as lower quality than the perceived speed of software.

Available

Available is an almost self-deprecating industry term for "working." Is the system "available"? I'm pretty sure this slang is from the early '90s, post generally available web, signifying if a resource can be reached via HTTP, but I don't have any authority on that. It's just common terminology nowadays for any service, API, or web-based product.

I partially place the suddenly super popular DORA metrics in the "Available" category to fit this quality context. What is DORA? DevOps Research and Assessment. This is what the DORA researchers say about themselves: "Our research team applies behavioral science methodology to uncover the predictive pathways which connect ways of working, via software delivery performance, to organizational goals and individual well-being."

And, of course, it's all Google people on behalf of Google. Which, by my limited definitions of importance in this book, and my previous book, *Patterns of Software Construction*, place DORA in the hard to achieve category for most development teams requiring multi year, deliberate work on culture, automation, and architecture. For example, why compare yourself to a professional athlete when you're just trying to jog out a couple of miles every Tuesday and Thursday?

So, in this case, some observers measure your quality in terms of operational tendencies of:

- Lead Time (to make a change to customers)
- Deployment Frequency (how often the software is deployed)
- Change Failure Percentage (particularly helpful)
- Recovery Time to Failed Deployment (now broke, now fixed)

Timely

Anyone involved with your software will want new features at a more frequent pace than you can accomplish, or they will want less change, and for you to release changes (features) slower. It is a paradox. Either way, timely new things are important to everyone.

All these views on quality sound good and fine until you decide to measure them yourself. Then, the academic, blog, and vendor favorite metrics become elusive. Chapter 5 goes into these areas in more detail.

More Security

Security goes into the list above, and in today's landscape, it occupies a special seat in the room too. You can build software, set up exceptional processes, have zero defects, and lose the entire business when hacked, breached, ransomed, and exposed. For instance, Toyota was breached in August 2024 when the "ZeroSevenGroup" stole 240GB of data, including financial and personal data on staff, customers, and network infrastructure. All while Toyota is held as a pinnacle of quality in their industry.

Failed security has a massive business impact. Corporations are spending significant parts of their budgets on security tools, policies, and preventative measures, and so is the US government and all other major world governments. There are cyber wars afoot across every major nation state and nefarious activity from the small ones who are trying to get a leg up and weaponize information systems into organized crime.

One breach dramatically drops the perceived quality of a product. The breach forces customers (especially business customers) to question the policies, procedures, development practices, and testing abilities of whom they are purchasing software from.

Locked Out

In 2024, Lurie Children's Hospital in Chicago suffered a months-long cyber security breach and lost personal data on nearly eight hundred thousand people. This was significant data: social security numbers, names, addresses, medical conditions, driver's license numbers, and prescription information. Basically everything.

The hackers locked Lurie out of all their systems, and the hospital had to intentionally take down their network to extricate the attackers at an eye-watering cost to their bank account and credibility.

This isn't just any hospital—Lurie Children's Hospital is the key research hospital for children in the Midwest. They perform lifesaving surgeries, procedures, and ongoing care that children cannot receive at other institutions. During the attack, and during the remediation phase, medical charts were offline and updates went manual to pen and paper; sometimes they didn't know how to dose a patient, which is a major cause of hospital mortalities in the US.

Our family had a patient at Lurie, and we were affected. She couldn't get the care she needed, but she was luckily not preparing for a significant procedure.

This didn't have to happen. They did not take their systems seriously—even though attacks on hospital systems were rising for years. They didn't focus on security as the key metric and therefore shattered all quality expectations.

Dependencies Increase Risk, but so Does Driving to the Store

In figure 1.2 below, there are six external dependencies to the application code. When dealing with enterprise-grade systems, this is a significantly conservative list of dependencies—it's going to be more. Product and engineering teams expect dependencies to always work—and that is a bad idea. Expecting dependencies to fail is a much more realistic mindset to take on, such as in figure 1.2 below.

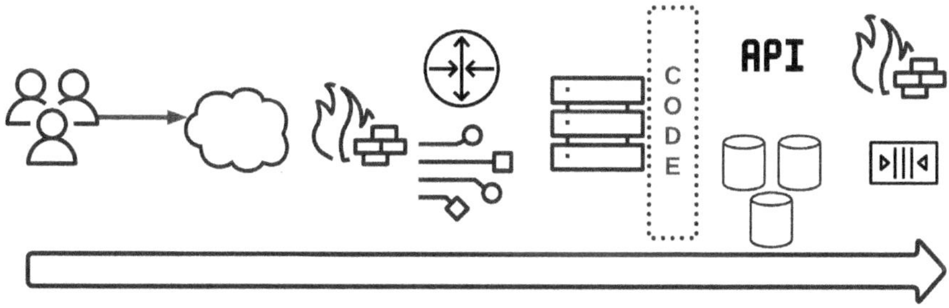

Figure 1.2 – Dependencies and complexity

The challenge is that modern applications are all dependencies. The alternative to this design is mainframes and minicomputers from the last century where the UI, data access, processing, and data are all integrated together. No one is going back to this world anytime soon.

Bad dependency management is a major cause of:

- Software system failures
- System security breaches
- Defects during development

Databases, authentication, APIs, and networking are all dependencies for the software you are building (the product) to work. To be more specific, the efficacy of your dependencies dictates the perceived quality of your new code investment.

If your dependencies fail, you fail.

Everything must work in unison, but it's not going to work all the time! The parts are going to fail, and managing this is very hard. If your transactions are expensive and valuable (like publishing the price of a mutual fund), the management of dependencies is more challenging than if the transaction is cheap and repeatable (updating the comment count on a social media message thread).

Dangers Abound

So, are dependencies dangerous? Yes. Statistically, driving to the grocery store is also dangerous. More car accidents happen within five miles of home than at any other point. This driving stat is interesting; people do more driving close to home than farther from home, so the chance for an accident is greater. So it's just a ratio, just math, and nothing magical.

It's the same with software dependencies—there are failures because we are using nearby software systems continuously, and those other systems (dependencies) have their own lifecycles. They are like other drivers—we don't know the details of what they are thinking or their focus. It becomes dangerous when we don't know what the other dependency will do and protect ourselves from severe damage.

There is no escaping these scenarios—it's the world we live in. But how do we manage it? We will get more into managing dependencies and its effect on quality in Chapter 4.

But It's Just a Dependency

Simple things can be dangerous. Too much fructose for a diabetic. Too much weight on bad knee.

Peanuts. Driving to the store. Crossing the street. Social media.

There are ways to manage all of these everyday dangers so they aren't so dangerous, if you take the time.

"Quality means doing it right when no one is looking." - **Henry Ford**

Customers, Clients, and Users

We can't even regulate ourselves.

This industry can't work together enough to create a shared vocabulary around those who are the users, clients, customers, and stakeholders. Think about it—tens of thousands of software projects running around the world, and every team defining what a user of their system is. (No one has agreement on the difference between a defect, bug, and issue, which we'll touch on in Chapter 2.)

There is nothing holding all this software running the world together. Yes, there are some certifications to achieve, but nothing is mandatory or consistent between companies and verticals. A team building software to process mortgage loans doesn't have anything in common with a team producing software to run refrigeration systems.

Every team, department, and company has its own definitions of who they think they are building software for. Before you think, well, these are just all customers, let's look at table 1.1 below where we define the categories.

Table 1.1 – Customer Categories

Name	Description	Location
Customer	Decision maker with budget.	External
Client	The company that has the customer.	External
User	The people who will use the software.	External
Stakeholder	Just about anyone ascribed interest in the project/outcomes.	Internal

This may appear salient on a brief glance. But the cause for concern is that those definitions can swap descriptions rapidly between teams and companies. Some teams call everyone not on the development team the "customer." Some companies refer to customers as clients and don't even use the term customer. It's not standard or rationalized across companies or teams, and this war is not worth fighting.

Note: It's a particularly nasty anti-pattern to call everyone who isn't on the product development team a customer. This is from a malady of agile in the early 2000s where every stakeholder was "served as a customer." This line of thinking is very off-base, because that's not how organizations function. If you are building software, the sales representative is not a customer. She is incentivized by very different outcomes than the development manager.

All in All

1. Not just an absence of defects (Chapter 2)
2. Quality is often political or emotional
3. Patterns and cultures affect reactions and perceptions of quality
4. Accepting "it's good enough"

What Is Software Engineering or Architecture Anyway?

The answer depends on who you ask.

In 2008, myself and a few other technical professionals in Chicago created a local user group focused on software architecture. We named it the Chicago Architects Group. It was a fun and exciting time until the cease-and-desist letter arrived from a trade group representing "real" architects—those who designed the buildings we were all meeting in. We didn't have any organization backing us up. The only organizations for software were academic—and they probably didn't care for us either, because we were practitioners. Eventually, we renamed the group the Chicago Information Technology Architects group, which was decidedly not as fun an experience.

So it turns out that even if those who build software daily don't have a consistent answer, other groups will happily tell us (or litigate) what software architecture and engineering is not.

Homogenous

The same software everywhere means the same defects and failures everywhere. Imagine if everyone in your geographic area, say ten square miles, had electric cars when the power grid fails for a week. It's going to look like an agrarian society by the time power is restored.

This is the same pattern that allows disease to wipe out entire populations.

A lack of variety allowed one problem from one vendor, like CrowdStrike, to take a ridiculous number of critical systems around the world offline.

What if Delta ran two software security detection systems? Put one vendor's software on all the workstations in airports, and the other software on the backend systems. Or, have two solutions, and divide up airports to use different solutions. That way, one bad change can't take down every terminal and gate at every single Delta location. At worst, it would take down half of them while the other travelers continue.

Part of a high-quality solution that does not cost extra is having the right diverse mix of technologies and staff. This is why dependencies aren't so bad—it alleviates the single point of total failure by producing multiple points of partial failure. Well, having more than one place to injure a critical system is better than the entire system going down all at once.

> The law of diminishing response: The more pressure you add, the less you get for it.

Many Good Choices Equals Success

Make good choices repeatedly and you will drop into the pit of success and deliver high-quality software. Quality is not elusive or expensive; instead, it requires consistency across many activities.

Summary

CrowdStrike posted a message from their CEO on their website during the outage recovery period, starting with, *"I want to sincerely apologize directly to all of you for the outage. All of CrowdStrike understands the gravity and impact of the situation. We quickly identified the issue and deployed a fix, allowing us to focus diligently on restoring customer systems as our highest priority..."*

That message is a flashing neon sign example of why focusing on quality first is the most important thing you can address on any software project.

CrowdStrike did not go down without a fight, and struck back at Delta. They pointed out that other airlines came back online days before Delta. And, with the tenacity of a boxer who had been hit enough, they pulled themselves from the ropes, inviting Delta to litigation because they had a contractual cap on monetary damages and Delta would have to disclose their IT problems to the world, allowing the courts and the public open examination of why Delta was offline for days while others using CrowdStrike recovered back to normal business operations.

Takeaway

Quality is not something else outside of the purview of software construction—it is software development itself.

Despite all the discourse and confusion about what a good software product is, you can describe it accurately and now know that you can capture quality, for free, inside what you have today. No extra fees are required. We will explore the challenges around defects in the next chapter.

2 – Considering Defects

John Carmack, considered the greatest programmer of all time, the author of the Doom Game Engine, was surprised how C++ developers at Facebook don't use IDE's or debuggers. During an interview on the Lex Freidman podcast, Friedman asked Carmack if he appreciated debuggers.

Carmack replied, "Very much so…a debugger is how you get a view into a system that's too complicated to understand. I mean, anybody that thinks (you can) just read the code and think about it—that's an insane statement; you can't even read all the code on a big system."

Carmack forgot more about how to write good code than most engineers learn in a lifetime. And he's spent a lifetime writing code to the metal, not fluffy abstractions inside some virtual runtime managing heaps and memory for you. He understands that perfect isn't best and pushing the edges sometimes means doing things that aren't pretty, but are effective.

You see, engineers and product development teams are forced into precarious positions on a regular basis regarding what others see as bugs or defects. Some complain that the "bug backlog" is too big, or that every unexpected thing a user does in a system is a "defect" —but alas, it's not that black and white.

Better Ways Forward

The way we think about defects in software isn't aligned toward the outcomes we want. Recording, managing, and resolving defects should improve the efficacy of the product and the customer experience. When defects become a misunderstood tool to beat teams up with, we have all lost.

All parties involved in the production of software want something that is void of problems, in other words perfect—and that is unrealistic at best and dangerous at worst. This chapter explores why this is and puts information in your hands to make decisions from new vantage points.

Bugs, Defects, Errors, and Failures

What is the difference between a bug, defect, error, and a failure? Let's review these concepts in table 2.1 below.

Table 2.1 – Categories of Issues

Category	Definition
Bug	The code performing a function the programmer did not mean for it to do.
Defect	A bug plus the diversion from a given requirement. This is the preferred term in many organizations.
Error	This is old terminology. Try to avoid it.
Failure	What customers experience directly or indirectly.

A primary concept to keep in mind is this: Bugs aren't moral. That is, having defects is not a moral issue. A programmer, Diego, who inadvertently generates two defects while implementing a feature is not judged to be either good or bad. Similarly, these two defects, as experienced in the software, and as recorded in the work item system, are not moral issues.

Seriously, note this, because there is a stigma often placed on the programmer to never fail. Often, QA managers or product managers refer to a list of defects in a pale and assuming manner, as if the neighbor's dog just did their business on their front steps. It's not moral, and it's certainly not ethical—it's just work. If it were possible to produce defect-free software on a regular basis, the industry would do so.

Defects are not a moral issue.

For instance, if my wife and I ordered a pizza with sausage, peppers, and onions, and the pizza came without the onions, our first reaction is not: "Those pizza people! They never listen to me! Now this is wrong, and I'm going to call everyone." Of course not. Because it's just a mistake. But why did they make the mistake? Because we ordered the pizza at 6 p.m. on Friday along with three hundred other families. The tickets are spitting out of the order printer faster than they can apply sauce to the dough.

Here is the distinction: In the pizza scenario, the customer (the person who eats the pizza) does not produce the requirements. The customer, me, told the pizza order taker what we wanted—and that's it. The pizza shop processes then take over—they write the functional requirements, along with the non-functional requirements (like being baked, hot) and give that to the pizza cooks. So, if the pizza arrives wrong, why would I be upset with the pizza cooks?

Defects Cost Money

Programmers don't start the day with the goal of creating defects, and it's not lost on anyone there are consequences to defects. Consequences are real—with actual monetary issues—when left undetected for too long. How long the defect is undetected is a measurement, though.

Let's look at another fictional example in table 2.2 below. Please keep in mind that the monetary figure is fictional and illustrative.

Table 2.2 – Impact on Customer Direct Use Software

Customer Facing Software (Revenue)		
Environment Where Defect Is Found	**Cost in Overall Impact to Project**	**Cost in $**
On the Developer's Machine	Nothing.	0
In Development	Business as usual.	1
In QA	Not much unless it's the same thing from development.	3
In Production (Live) with Users	Massive.	100

Figure 2.1 below illustrates how costs trend versus software hosting environments. It starts with local, then development, followed by a QA environment and finally production. Do you see how those figures went completely non-linear?

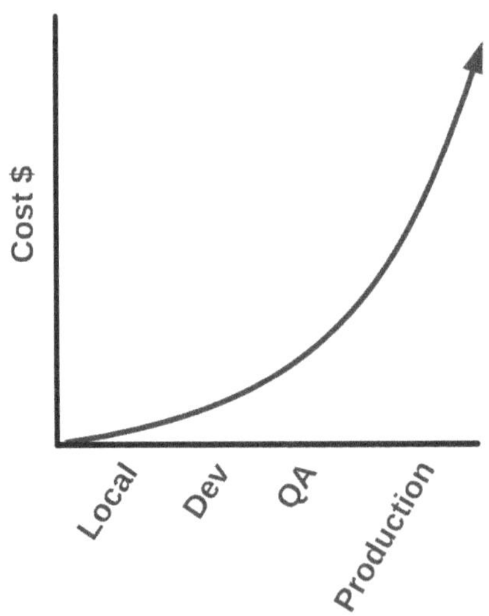

Figure 2.1 – Non-linear correlations of cost to environments

Now, this only matters if the software is sold to generate revenue. In many cases, as outlined in my previous book, *Patterns of Software Construction*, and as we visit in Part 2 with the LIFT Engineering System, portions of teams building software don't have any "paying" customers. This doesn't mean the work isn't important! (There are many internal systems, that in fact, seem useless.) Mission critical systems power our world—and they are used by "operators." Flight control systems, health care, oil and gas, energy, etc. Table 2.3 below outlines the cost of issues for these kinds of systems—and it tends to maintain linearity.

Table 2.3 – .Critical System Issue Costs

Internal Facing Software of Non-Mission-Critical-System		
Environment Where Defect Is Found	**Cost in Overall Impact to Project**	**Cost in $**
On the Developer's Machine	Nothing.	0
In Development	Business as usual.	0
In QA	Business as usual.	1
In Production (Live) with Users	A little more than business as usual.	10

These are illustrations to help you think about defects, quality, and customers. The dollar figures expressed are fabricated to help illustrate the story. In both cases, internal and external customer-facing systems, the impact to project delivery, and the cost measured in dollars is exponential from a defect caught in development versus the same defect found in production.

Why is the defect so much more expensive when caught in production?

When a defect is found in production, it costs more to fix than one found in development for many reasons. First, identifying, diagnosing, and reproducing the defect in the production environment may take more time and effort than in the development, as the production environment may have different configurations, data, or dependencies.

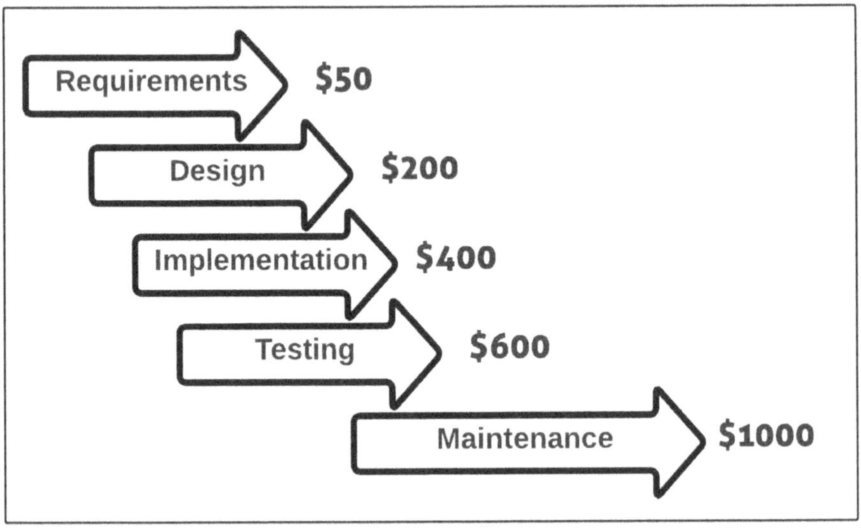

Second, the defect may have a negative impact on the customer's use of the software, accuracy, trust, and retention, as well as the reputation of the product or service provider, which may result in loss of revenue, market share, or competitive advantage. In short, customers don't hate defects—they hate software that becomes useless. In this case, the software could be free, but it's still not worth having, because it doesn't work.

Third, the defect may expose the product or service provider to legal, regulatory, or contractual liabilities. These can be as varied as fines, penalties, or lawsuits, which may include additional costs and damages. The production defect can also breach service level agreements, which can lead to hard conversations at the minimum and more lawsuits in severe cases.

Fourth, deploying a patch or a workaround to the production system may require additional resources and coordination, as well as careful planning and testing, to minimize the disruption and downtime for the customers and users. It's simpler to design, build, test, and deploy an individual feature during early software development phases when the system has a complexity level of three out of ten versus when the system is fully baked with a complexity level of seven out of ten.

Fifth, fixing the defect may divert the attention and focus of the development team from working on new features or enhancements, which may delay the delivery of value to customers. These crisis activities siphon time away from additional development efforts—instead of working on the next release, some team members, including management, are wrapped up in the last release. This is true debt—constantly fixing the past instead of moving into the future. It's like paying the minimum balance on a credit card and watching the balance grow from interest. This kind of life for a product development and engineering team is demoralizing and suffocating.

Therefore, it is much more cost-effective and beneficial for team health to prevent and resolve defects as early as possible in the development process rather than waiting until they are discovered in production.

> "The best way to handle defects is not to make them in the first place."

Then everything is a defect!

Some team members enter bugs into the backlog as if they are going to win a participation trophy. Every pixel, every decimal, everything that confuses them or they're unsure of—every everything. Well, it may not be worthwhile.

Writing a defect into a backlog doesn't mean it is:

1. A defect, or

2. A bug, or
3. Anything at all

A possible reality exists where the supposed defect is, in fact, just an observation.

It's a dirty little secret that only developers and some smart managers understand—defect backlogs are nonsense. Anyone can enter anything anytime—which makes many of those entries nonsense at best and time-wasting, money-gobbling messes at worst.

Let's say I'm picking apples on a beautiful autumn day. I pick a nice red one and place it in the basket. I pick a green one and put it in the basket. Now someone comes running up the field, flailing their arms, yelling, "Wait, overnight we picked all of these things, and we want to put them in the basket!" They empty a bag of items into my apple basket. But they're not apples. Some are bananas, some are pears, and some are peanut butter and jelly sandwiches.

I say, "Thanks? These aren't apples and this is an apple basket. What am I supposed to do with all this?" and they reply, "They are bugs. You must review all of them!"

And that is how the morning starts for the development team—reviewing a backlog of half-nonsense from testing. This is the defect backlog of the modern organization.

"If he gets up, we all get up—it's anarchy!" – ***The Breakfast Club,* 1985**

Hurrah, no defects!

Having a hundred defects for every ten features released to production may indicate a problem in either the development process or the testing process.

Few people would argue this empirical viewpoint of quality across a given set of features.

> An absence of defects says nothing about quality.

Software is like anything else in life. My neighbors' house may look like it's worth a cool million bucks—until you look in the basement. It's damp. It's dark. Its sump pump pit overflows with water every six months during moderate rain. It's not a big deal to the owner; they just let it dry out. Even with all this, there is no case of reported mold in the basement or the house. And everyone goes on as if their world is sunny and happy.

That is, until that house goes on the market and a prospective buyer hires a professional who measures the mold count in the basement with the right set of tools. Now, there is evidence of mold—that is, evidence of existence.

Of course, it could go the other way too—the testing could find nothing. But not finding mold doesn't mean it doesn't exist—it just means no one found it. The original homeowner was living in a non-factual fantasy, believing the lack of evidence of mold (i.e., not seeing mold spores) meant mold did not exist. This was dangerous for the homeowner, and it's dangerous in software.

> Having abundant defects does guarantee useless software, but having zero defects guarantees nothing about the value of the software.

We can rephrase this as: A lot of flaws will make software worthless, but no flaws will not make software valuable. Why? Because quality is not just zero defects. Quality is the combination of the entire system: its usage and all the components and dependencies that go into it. Imagine a simplified view of a normal SaaS business system in 2025.

We have network infrastructure like routers, switches, and WANs. We have APIs built purposefully for the application, databases, and various dependencies that can come in many forms (API, message queue, file systems), and finally, something running the application code! The code may run on a virtual machine, bare metal, as a serverless function, inside of containers (docker, AKS, Kubernetes) or something not yet invented.

It may not be the code

Stepping back and looking at the entire system, a system view, quality may be perceived through the lenses of incidents. If you're not familiar with incidents, it is the phrase *du jour* of SaaS/IT over the last decade as a default wrapper for any problem with systems, customers, data, or anything else that impedes anyone doing anything, anywhere, at any time of day. If the app is down, it's an incident. If the data is wrong, it's an incident. It's an incident before teams can triage the issue and decide if there is a real bug or if it's just a network switch failing somewhere.

But, through the tyranny of populist technologists wanting everyone to be a generalist, we have melded parts of the technology stacks together that don't need gluing. Last to say, and at the case of sounding repetitive, the problem may not be the code.

Defect Runaway

When defects run away, the likelihood of losing quality increases significantly. Why? Because compounding defects decreases the usefulness of the software, like in figure 2.2.

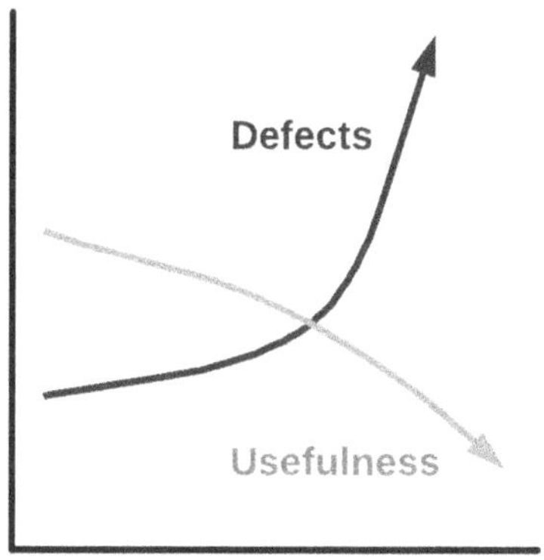

Figure 2.2 – Defects up, usefulness down

So how many defects can your product tolerate? Are five hundred defects okay? Are one thousand okay? How about one hundred thousand? Whatever number you land on is driven by perception and subjectivity, which makes its measurement non-analytical.

No matter the number you choose, as already discussed, people will disagree with you. The trend is what you must control; when defects "run" away, problems arise. When defects slowly build up, it's manageable business as usual.

Who cares anyway?

Stakeholders during software builds love to zero in on defects because they are easily seen. But only the engineers know what's really happening. They know if the buildup of bad technical decisions is going to topple the product like a Jenga tower, exploding pieces all over the table and the floor. This is why teams spend more time focusing on overall quality and not just a list of seemingly random and disconnected items.

You can't control the unknown. You can just manage the risk. In the book *The Black Swan,* Nassim Nicholas Taleb discusses several key principles related to unpredictability and randomness:

1. **Swan Events**: Taleb describes these as highly improbable events that have massive impacts on society and are often rationalized with hindsight as if they could have been expected.

2. **Non-Predictability**: The book emphasizes the limitations of our ability to predict black swan events due to their rare and unpredictable nature.

3. **Robustness:** Taleb advocates for building systems and approaches that are robust to negative events and can benefit from positive ones.

4. **Narrative Fallacy**: Humans tend to create stories post-event to make sense of these events, which can mislead our understanding of randomness.

5. **Confirmation Bias**: We often focus on what confirms our existing knowledge while ignoring what contradicts it.

6. **Silent Evidence**: Taleb points out the tendency to consider only the visible successes while ignoring the "silent" ones that did not make it.

The book advises against the human tendency to simplify and categorize complex events. He calls us to be aware of the limitations of our knowledge and prepare for the unexpected.

Selection Fallacy

Have you ever gone apple picking in the fall? Imagine a crisp autumn day, where the sun is sitting at that fall height, bathing everything in an orange-red glow, and the temperature is enough to call for coats but not gloves. You walk through the rows of trees, carrying a basket, deciding which apples to pluck and drop in your container. No one just stops and takes thirty apples and leaves. No way. We pick each one carefully, with thought, determined to get the best.

The sad fact is, we don't know anything about the variety of apples in the orchards. And whatever is picked, if good, is nothing but luck. How we look at our defects generates just as much selection bias.

1) Analyzing all your defects across all projects to determine some kind of trend while not considering projects that failed or were cancelled.

2) Choosing customer support tickets to be the same as confirmed software defects. Some users may not report them, because they have workarounds. Others may report everything.

3) Backward observations: when the product manager and engineering director are excited about a new release being high quality when there are few changes and few users touching them to report problems. Of course, there aren't any reported defects—nothing changed, and no one is using it!

4) Using code pull requests as a sign of technical reviews (nothing must happen except clicking approve).

"Quality is not an act; it is a habit." - **Aristotle**

Defect Detection Curve

Welcome to the defect detection curve in figure 2.4 below, demonstrating the defects hardest to find are in fact found last. This explains why the "we're 99 percent complete" paradigm occurs while a non-stop, long-running slew of defects slowly rolls in. It's like watching a barge come down the river—it moves so slow you barely see it moving, but eventually it's right in front of you, and it's huge.

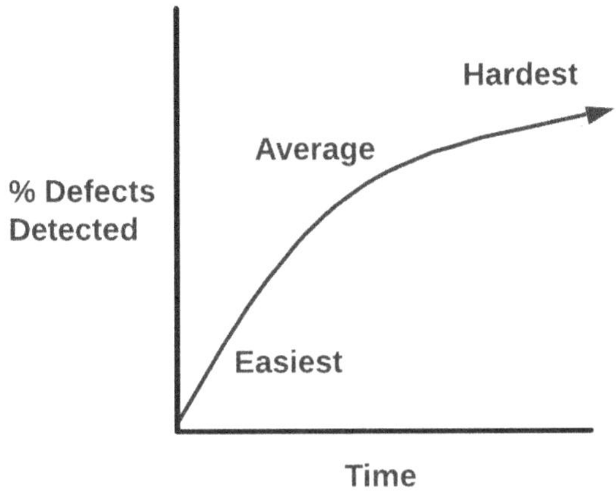

Figure 2.3 – Defect Detection Curve

There is no testing methodology or tool that can find detects in a linear manner. Therefore, the smallest amount of the test time is spent on a few easy problems, and most of the easy problems are found early in the test cycle. This is not helpful.

Consider:

- The easiest-to-find defects are found first.
- The hardest-to-find will be detected last.
- Therefore, the average detection time will keep rising throughout the project.

Now, see figure 2.4 below and how these defect detection times prolong over time.

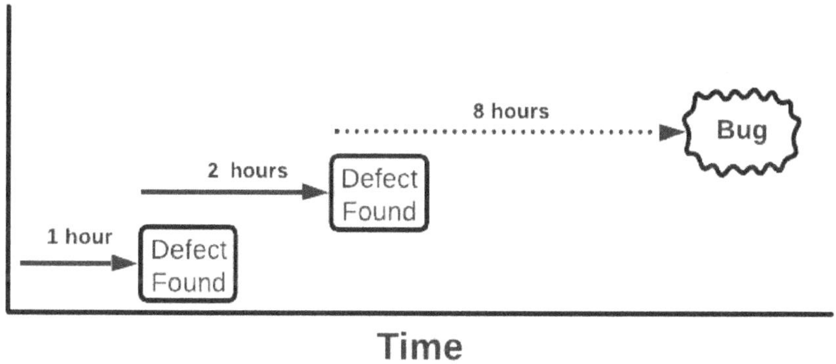

Figure 2.4 – Defect Detection Prolongment

Estimates Are Linear

Estimates tend to be made using linear expectations and projections.

Humans believe the time it takes to find the last defects will be the same time to find the next set, but only if we are still in the easy zone (see above). When moving into the average or hardest zones, the time will increase. We believe if it takes thirty minutes to find the first set of defects, the next set will take thirty. This is a poor assumption (though optimistic). It took sixty minutes to find the next set, so we think the next will take sixty minutes, but in fact it will take a hundred minutes, and onward.

The non-linear behavior of finding defects in systems is a major factor in managing quality and one we must take account of.

Summary

- Organizations struggle with defects because they conceptualize them incorrectly.
- Defects are not moral issues.
- The absence of defects reported says nothing about the quality of a system.
- Not all system problems are defects.
- The defect detection curve states that not all defects can be found in the same amount of time.

Takeaway

Defects have consequences, but they are not the pinnacle of all conversations and tradeoffs in quality.

When John Carmack wrote the original Doom Game Engine, it had defects—and he made decisions and tradeoffs that still made the game the most consequential advancement in PC gaming ever. He didn't wait until it was defect-free to be successful; instead, the function of the software spoke for itself and changed the world. He knew, and still knows now, it was not possible to write something as complex as that engine without defects.

Now that you understand where defects should fit into the overall concern and quality of software, we'll explore the characteristics of decision making in the next chapter.

3 – Dialing in Decisions

"Show me the incentive and I'll show you the outcome." - **Charlie Munger**

Every year 3.1 million students start college as a freshman. That means that there are 3.1 million students who had to decide which school to join.

One of them, Janice Archer, achieved a 3.8 on her high school GPA leading up to her senior year, so she wasn't too concerned about getting into a college. She enjoyed her English courses more than she thought she would and started writing short stories on her own. *The Eaton Town Journal* even published one of her stories last spring. Her friends on the basketball team always found this amusing, since Janice was their leading scorer and a few colleges told their coach their intention to watch her play in the fall.

And sure enough, the first Tuesday in October, UVW and UNLV showed up to Janice's second home game, where she scored twenty-two points, had four assists, and three rebounds. The next day, the UVW recruiter called her parents and asked for a meeting that Friday, which, after consulting with Janice, they accepted.

Meanwhile, Janice received a letter in the mail from Eaton College of the Arts. She opened the envelope, and inside was an invitation to come study literature at Eaton College along with a $40,000 annual discount while she maintained a 3.8 GPA. Her excitement was as powerful as the bemusement of the letter—as she never applied. The college saw her story published in their literature journal from a high school student and decided to make her the offer without an application.

She senses a basketball scholarship is around the corner—but now she can study something she loves somewhere that could be amazing. What should Janice do?

In this chapter, you will learn how software systems are the consequence of human interactions, and the outcome of those interactions are decisions. Sometimes this is for the best, and sometimes not. When you learn ways to step back and look at decisions, you can create the space required to improve your decision-making around design, planning, and overall quality. You have a limited amount of decision-making fuel everyday—don't waste it on trivial things.

Dead Men Tell No Tales

It is easy to judge other people's decisions.

I think, "She made a great decision" when the decision yields good results for me.

We say, "That was an awful decision!" when the decision yields results we don't want.

And people cry out, "They just messed it up for all of us" when any politician makes any decision, about anything, anywhere, ever.

First, it's not healthy to criticize others when our house is a mess—it ends up hurting everyone. Second, decisions are contextual, not static, so we are never familiar with the information someone had when deciding (even the politicians).

Let's pretend there are two people who must decide what technology to use for a new data project: Decision Maker A and Decision Maker B. Additionally, we have someone else watching the decision-making, whom we call the Observer, who doesn't have knowledge of the details of each decision maker's environment.

Decision Maker A's environment is extremely complex—networking components, products, existing systems, skillsets, various teams, political maneuvering, training schedules, leader buy-in, existing contracts, and budget constraints.

Decision Maker B's environment is simple. They have one SaaS product, one product manager, three engineers, and one cloud hosting service.

They both decide to license the *Koopa Data Integration* product after an analysis period. It took Decision Maker A three months to decide, and Decision Maker B decided in two weeks.

The Observer watching Decision Maker A is perplexed that it took them months to make a simple decision. Subsequently, the Observer high fives and sends a warm email to Decision Maker B for their rapid decision.

Is this fair? No. Did Decision Maker A do something wrong? Why did it take A ten weeks longer than B to make the same decision?

Here is an illustration of each decision maker's environments.

Decision Maker A's environment is so much more complex than B's environment that of course the decision timeline was longer for A. For one, A had to talk to more humans—it wasn't a singular care of finding the right fit. Second of many reasons, Decision Maker B ended up buying three licenses for a total of $2,200 on a credit card. Meanwhile, Decision Maker A purchased 150 licenses for $120,000 after a lengthy corporate procurement process.

Apples and Oranges

Tiny companies with three developers don't have a CTO who leads them. It's really a lead developer—no matter how desperately that individual wants to attend events and wear a name badge that says CTO. It's like an entrepreneur who re-sells video games online calling themselves a CEO—they are not a chief executive, or officer, of anything. If you don't believe it, watch reruns of Shark Tank sometime; they give it straight to the entrepreneur.

Prestigious authors and researchers write large treatises and scholarly books on decision-making—so don't let this little aside replace in-depth research. I'm simply addressing the idea that making decisions isn't straightforward, and there are reasons why we are where we are in anything.

Our marriage is the way it is because we don't spend time together.

My bank account is how it is because I don't use a budget.

The file import system on the team is the way it is because people made decisions. And not simply a few decisions—hundreds if not thousands of decisions, all attempting to use the best information available while the complexity around them increased. After all, we can't use information that we don't have. Sure, another team may have knowledge of something we don't, but if we don't know it, it's not baked into the calculus for the decision we're making now.

Keep in mind, failing businesses don't have a chance to become complex. So, running into what you consider odd decisions may be a sign that someone, to everyone's utter disbelief, may have done something right. After all, dead men tell no tales.

Decision Factors

Working in software means constant change. Requirements advance, systems change, teams change, and business grows or falls like leaves from a fall tree, withering, slowly, until they are gone. Salespeople learned that you don't have to say yes to every request, but you shouldn't give a hard no either. Trend towards yes and leave the no for someone else to share. That is how deals are done.

Avoid saying no to everything request, change, or feature that comes in.

Don't say yes to it all either.

There is a spectrum for saying yes and when to say no. Figure 3.1 below shows how we learn *when* to yes and *when* to say no over your career.

Figure 3.1 – Novice to Expert

Someone young and early in their career needs to gain experience, so when they are asked to do something, they should trend toward saying yes. Saying no too often closes doors that they won't even know require opening later in their career.

On the other side of the timeline are experts. An expert has different motivations; it took them many years and effort to gain their expertise, and their desire is to keep their status and success. In their case, they learned to say no, nicely, over time. They didn't become an expert in a field by doing everything, and their specialty is special because of the time they continue investing.

What does this have to do with quality engineering or software? Well, new systems need people to say yes to build features for revenue generation and then, later, to say yes less, so they can keep making money and keep margins healthy. Saying yes less means saying no sometimes. Figure 3.2 below shows how experience and the yes/no answer correlate over time.

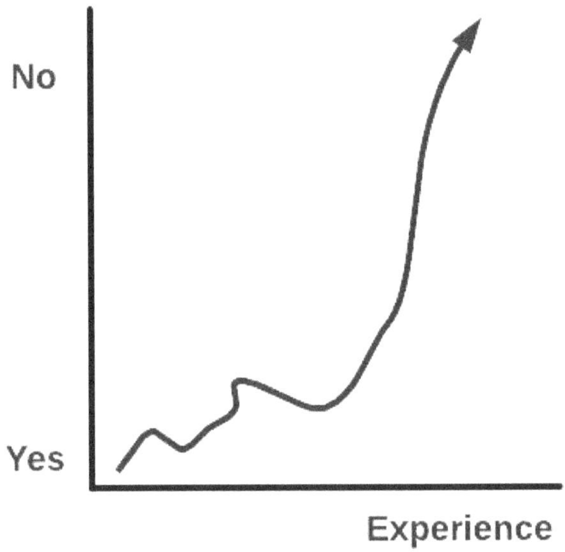

Figure 3.2 – Experience Means Saying No

Toyota

Business book authors are overly keen on referencing Toyota and their legendary efficiency. So, tough luck, business school folks, because the tech industry has been Toyota enthusiasts for at least the last twenty-five years with the adoption of Lean principles. Though, I guess, sometimes people just want to scream Kaizen! Or reference Andon Cords (like I have earlier in the book). So let's get into it. The Toyota Way has a list of fourteen principles…with number one being:

Base your management decisions on a long-term philosophy, even at the expense of short-term financial goals.

Let's simplify it. It's better to sacrifice short-term financial gains to meet the long-term goals.

Hmm. That's still not simple enough. How about:

Survive now, win later.

Waterfalls Move Water

Leaders decide how to plan software repeatedly because the process is never ending. Nowadays, everyone just fights about what planning means, what sprints means, what iterations means—it's just a waste of time. Wasting your decision resources on this topic is silly, and I'll prove it.

Twenty-five years ago, we ran software projects with the waterfall methodology, and we called it waterfall. Today, we do waterfall, but we call it agile.

Teams think they are very advanced—but a culling is in waiting. Managing Jira (the almost default development management tool by Atlassian) user stories is not agile. Grooming backlogs is not agile. It's expensive, and there is no quantitative proof agile ceremonies improve overall software quality at scale. The biggest winners don't follow scripts—they write them. If you want to generate $30 million in revenue, you steal the team from fruitless busy work and focus on developing features (to sell), quality (to retain customers), and unique functionality (to generate a moat). No one says, "Our focus as a business is running scrum."

No, sorry. The traditional Agile coach relishes telling (coaching) an entire enterprise, CEO down, that adopting agile thinking is the only way to win in today's economy. But why do they think this? Because Agile became it's own business.

Decisions Are Nothing but Tradeoffs

"I'd like some pizza, but I don't really want the carbs." So get chicken parmesan—lots of sauce and cheese, with low carbs. That's a good tradeoff.

"I want the fastest app on the planet, but it also has to have more features per square inch of screen real estate than other competitors." Well, be ready for some tradeoffs.

"Give me the predictability of a structured, planned schedule, but also allow plenty of emergent design so we are fluid." Yep, more tradeoffs.

Let's unpack this last example. When you engage in structured, planned design, you receive predictability and some standard reporting that makes stakeholders feel warm and fuzzy. But you can miss opportunities as they emerge or use new information appropriately. On the other hand, teams that rely on only emergent design tend to have less predictable releases and major problems managing budgets.

These tradeoffs are compelling enough to review before starting projects and ruefully considering how one tradeoff versus the other allows for a greater share of quality in the end product. Figure 3.3 below shows two of these examples.

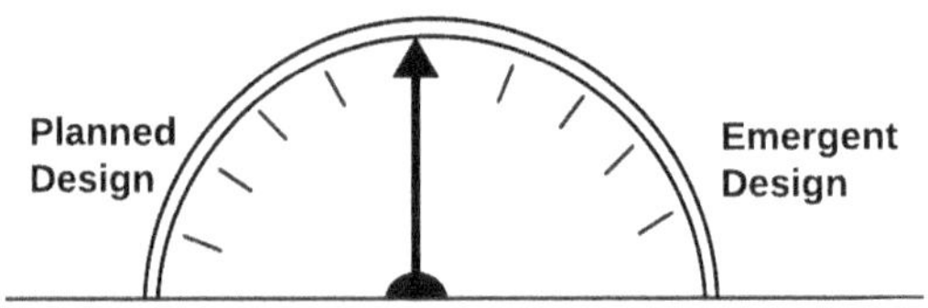

Figure 3.3 – Planned vs Emergent Design

The easier place to witness the quality tradeoffs is with the constant discussion of quality versus performance. This is simple, though.

Sacrificing quality for performance gets neither.

Stated differently, low quality cannot be highly performant in nature, because it doesn't work. A race car can't have broken parts and set speed records. Amazon can't have the fastest checkout in the industry and drop one out of every ten orders. The dissonance radiates loudly. In the end, evaluating tradeoffs is a classic part of claiming quality in systems.

Neuroscience and Group Think: The Gregory Burns Study

A neuroscientist named Gregory Burns conducted a 2005 study utilizing MRI scanners to explore how the human brain responds in situations involving social group think. Burns aimed to determine whether individuals who conformed to group opinions did so while still internally knowing the correct answer, or if their actual perceptions were altered by the influence of the group.

Researchers observed that when individuals agreed with a group providing incorrect answers, there was increased activity in brain regions associated with spatial awareness. This suggests that group responses can influence participants' perceptions of what they see or know. Therefore, errors made by others may affect how a person perceives the external world.

The Addition Principal

When I was young, we had a nice yard with lots of bushes and trees separating us from the neighbors. This coverage invited wildlife that my kindhearted mother enjoyed. She would give extra food scraps to possums or racoons. The food also attracted cats—which is to say, more cats, as we already had our own cats. Sometimes a feral cat would be friendly and hang around the lot, and we bonded. One of these cats, which we just called "Black-black" in that "singsongy" way, because, well, he was black, was a favorite. Sadly, one day he turned up with a large wound on his face that required a new experience for Black-black: a veterinarian visit.

We attracted him into the garage, and then into a corner so that coaxing him into a pet carrier might become somewhat doable, and can you guess what happened? He lashed out. Not just once, but multiple times, stuck in a loop. Sharp claws. Fangs. You could smell his fear and see it in the upright fur on his back. Trying to pick him up just led to more clawing. There had to be a better way.

Next, my mother in all her wisdom said he was hungry, as he'd been gone for a while, hence the wound, and we should leave the food in the carrier. No more talking or distracting—just leave the food and wait. We waited, he entered the pet carrier, and we quickly shut the door and latched it shut.

My mother had us change tactics, thank goodness. I kept doing the same thing, grabbing the cat and trying to put him in the carrier. And the cat was consistent too—fighting.

We act like this all the time building software systems; we keep doing the same thing repeatedly. For instance, when planning a release, we follow the same set steps that produce change failures in production, but we keep following the same operational steps repeatedly. The Addition Principle states that you can reduce ineffective behavior by adding more effective behavior. So, instead of taking the same steps as last release, creating a change failure, you should add a new step in your process that yields fewer change failures. Then, do that again and again without the concern of removing steps. Don't remove anything—just add.

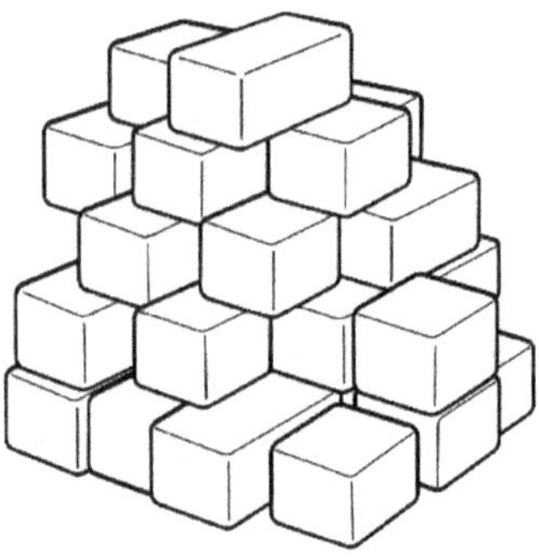

Why shouldn't you create a new process or remove steps and replace them? Because changing a system is hard, while adding to an existing system is easier. Think about it like a stack of blocks. Removing a block from anywhere in the stack, except the very top, will create structural integrity issues. The stack may shake or rattle or topple over. Or how about swapping a block for another block—this may be even harder to accomplish. Now, add a block to the top—the pile stands. Indeed, you can often get away with adding numerous blocks to the top before you run into integrity issues—so keep adding until the shaking starts.

Prefer adding behavior over changing or removing behavior.

Decisions Are Hard in Fictional Reality

My wife is a talented interior designer with a specialty in color and paint. She can identify between shades of white and identify, somewhat objectively, before the white becomes gray. It's not an easy skill, but she is talented. Clients ask, "Is that wall white or gray?" and she'll defer to responding with "Do you like the shade?" or "Which would you prefer, white or gray?" She converses with clients on paint selections like this example because she understands that everyone lives in their own reality created from a life of experiences, and that every decision they make in the design process with her was contextualized somewhere.

People behave from their model of the world, not from an objective reality.

Product People Can't Make All the Product Decisions

Have you ever heard of an NGO, or non-governmental organization? These are groups like Oxfam, the Nature Conservancy, or the AARP. Instead of the government trying to run departments that support wildlife, retired people or international human rights, it partners through funding with these organizations. It delegates decision-making to the NGO as a supporter. It can also, through funding, influence the activities of a given NGO toward the government's current interests.

Everyone has interests. But not everyone has the same knowledge or skillsets.

It's as simple as passing the bread at the dinner table to delegate all decision making to a requirements team, which as of this writing, is generally the practice of product management. Product managers are tasked with understanding the market fit, the customer experience, product requirements, and go-to market strategy. With agile ideas, the product managers also became indirect pseudo-development team leaders, sometimes working out well and at other times stagnating results with layers of prioritization and confusion. Teams end up with someone embedded in the team doing two things that cannot be done alone in a vacuum without developers.

1. Producing all requirements (functional and non-functional)
2. Prioritizing and sequencing work

"Product owners can't be the only ones making product decisions. Why? Because they don't understand the structure of the code."

Imagine a complex financial trading system, even though its complexity means you can't imagine it! Okay, this system is built over the last ten years with more rules than anyone can imagine built into the system. A new product manager, Joseph, wants to provide analysis of the past ten days of trades for each customer based on a new statistical algorithm. Joseph writes up ten user stories, drops them in the backlog, and pats himself on the back. Job well done!

Indeed.

This work is not doable, because it makes assumptions about the system that aren't false but aren't valid. You must understand if you've built software (code), the structure of the code is everything. Literally everything.

So prudent teams, building non-trivial systems, field requirements from developers too. That increases the odds of success significantly. A fast-food hamburger may hit the spot sometimes—but the burger from the gastropub will knock your socks off!

Ignoring the Past

Ignoring the past can be a bad idea for several reasons. First, the past is a valuable source of information that can help us make better decisions in the present. By studying the past, we can learn from the successes and failures of those who came before us and apply those lessons to our own lives. For example, by studying the history of pandemics, we can learn how to better prepare for future outbreaks and prevent them from becoming global catastrophes.

Second, ignoring the past can lead to a distorted view of reality. When we ignore the past, we risk repeating the same mistakes repeatedly. This can lead to a cycle of negative outcomes that could have been avoided if we had learned from the past.

Third, ignoring the past can prevent us from understanding the present. The past shapes who we are today, and by ignoring it, we risk missing important contexts that can help us understand the world around us. For example, by studying the history of political systems, we can better understand the current state of politics and the challenges we face as a society.

Finally, ignoring the past can prevent us from appreciating the progress we have made. By studying the past, we can see how far we have come and appreciate the hard work and sacrifices of those who came before us. This can inspire us to continue making progress and work toward a better future.

In conclusion, ignoring the past can have serious consequences. By studying the past, we can learn from the successes and failures of those who came before us, avoid repeating the same mistakes, understand the present, and appreciate the progress we have made. It's important to remember that the past is not something to be ignored or forgotten, but rather something to be studied and learned from.

Design Decisions

The design of software is just decisions, and it's incredibly hard. It was hard in the 1970s, and it's just as hard, probably even harder, today. There is no subjective right in writing code, but there is a subjective wrong. Code linters and static analysis point out the problems with code easily and regularly, but they aren't sophisticated enough to address if a whole system design is accurate or good, let alone "great."

The work of achieving the right investment mix of ideas to code structure leads to constraints that only developers of the system understand. Our trusty product manager, Joseph, can ask Sarah what the code structure constraints are, but they won't make sense. Holding the mental model of a software component and its dependencies in your head is a 4D model that doesn't lend itself well to words, because you must use the code to explain the code.

If you don't want your answer in C++, don't ask the question.

A Dollar In, a Dollar Out

Well, not quite. It turns out losing a dollar hurts more than winning a dollar. Daniel Kahneman and Amos Tversky introduced the concept of loss aversion in 1979. Through their research they found people strongly favored avoiding losses over attaining the equivalent sums. This could go for anything—not just money. Losing a cow from the herd hurts more than the gain of winning a cow in a contest.

Why this concept is true is moot—it just is. So, teams wish to avoid losing. To do so, companies do a couple different things.

1. Push feature delivery (revenue) into the future and pull all the software design expense to now. This often leads to losing all their money and going out of business.

2. They can do all the design work later, make some money, and then fight the poor design decisions in years three through five.

Quality design reduces the cost of making software; therefore, good decisions lead to good design—and good design leads to good decisions: a virtuous cycle.

Summary

Even with all the decisions requiring time and attention, you can make effective decisions by dialing them in. In this chapter, you saw when to analyze decisions, when to say no, and how any decision is better than no decisions. When you become paralyzed, think about that stack of blocks—don't pull a block out; instead, put another on top.

Takeaway

What did Janice do? She waited another week, received the basketball scholarship, and studied writing at the same time. She didn't trade writing for basketball, nor did she trade basketball for writing—she waited just a little longer, and her options were better than ever.

Dialing in decisions is critical to where you go in the quality journey because decisions are all we have. In the next chapter, we'll cover why simplifying processes and systems produces higher quality and longer-term results.

4 - Slow and Simple

Growing up, I loved the Indiana Jones movies *Raiders of the Lost Ark, The Temple of Doom,* and *The Last Crusade. Raiders of the Lost Ark* has one of the most famous scenes in movie history—a giant boulder thundering down a corridor to crush anything in its path as Indy runs away for his life, avoiding threats and leaping over obstacles. It's classic movie fun. But there was more to that scene I loved than that final action. I admired how Indy entered the cave with his cautious yet confident steps toward securing the treasure—in this case, a golden idol—and escaped with his life and the statue. Let me take you back.

Indiana Jones pans into the scene, his guides exhausted and thirsty, arriving at a dark cave set in the side of a damp, hot Amazon jungle. Two of the guides observe a dark omen marked on a tree and depart posthaste. It's now just Indiana and one guide. They enter the cave cautiously, on the lookout for traps and danger. Indiana notes human skulls, bones, old arrowheads, a wide chasm to cross, and other important items as they move through the space. Indiana, Dr. Jones, is a smart operator and is planning his escape as he progresses. Finally, they arrive at an arched room with the golden idol thirty yards ahead, sitting upon a dais. The guide makes to sprint forward, but Jones grabs him and urges patience. Indiana, using a large, ancient, unlit wooden torch, pushes some of the floor tiles until arrows are released and slam into the torch, protecting Indiana. Now, he steps carefully forward until he's arrived at the golden statue.

The statue can't be any more than ten by eight inches, all gold and shining brilliantly. Indiana's eyes sparkle with anticipation. He removes a leather pouch and fills it with sand, adding some, removing some, to estimate a swap on the dais for the statue. His travels have informed this experience to be wary of weight-based alarms. Finally, after much sweating analysis, Indiana swaps the bag of sand for the idol.

After a moment, he smiles back at his guide. The ruse worked—the dais remains in the same place, none the wiser from the statue's removal. Another moment passes. And the stone supporting the bag of sand sinks into the dais while the cave starts collapsing—the trick did not work! Indiana and his guide sprint for their lives out of the room.

Indiana faced many challenges on the way out, including shooting arrows, the chasm, a treacherous guide, and the massive stone ball tracking him down as he leaps from the cave. He makes it out alive because he spent time analyzing the cave, making note of details so that if something went wrong, his chance of exit, and his survival, would increase. Indiana Jones prepared. He took the time to understand the variables at play.

Indiana Jones went slow so that later he could go fast. He kept things simple. And these decisions allowed him to generate enough velocity to escape the cave alive with the treasure.

When you make the effort to prepare and simplify, you can go fast later. If you just try to go fast from the start, complexity mounts, and you risk a meltdown, or worse: an explosion with collateral damage.

Slow You

So what does slowing down mean? Does this mean just do the same things at a reduced pace? Yes. But also, no.

The first approach is to slow down as an individual—that means you and your behaviors; however, these techniques are far outside the scope of this text, as this is not a self-improvement book. In practice, we often see the scenario play out with a VP or director setting a tone with stakeholders, moving at a sustainable cadence for themselves and taking deliberate steps to ensure the team is observing their stable pace.

Meet Margot: she is the director of engineering for the Fluxometer Corporation. They make the best fluxometers in the world, and Margot's team is responsible for the firmware going into the third generation product line. She is excited for the opportunity to lead the development of such a critical part of the company's overall business—but she's also concerned with the scope of the project.

Additionally, she has to contend with stakeholders from all over the organization, like Samantha, the VP of customer excellence. Samantha's team burned themselves out during the release of the generation two fluxometer with a non-stop customer support issue during the rollout, and she has publicly stated on numerous occasions that "we are never releasing like that again." Margot already has six status meetings on her calendar from Samantha's team. On top of that, she has to deal with existing software vendors, new team members, and a slew of other jealous directors who wanted to run the project.

There is pressure to show results quickly so sales can commit to sales numbers in Q1 of the following year. Her instincts tell her to run fast and show results. But running fast right away is the wrong choice.

Instead, Margot slows down. She cancels the "Sprint Planning Meeting" the product management team scheduled with her thirty developers.

"Why did you cancel our meeting?" Stew, product management VP, asks Margot.

Margot replies, "Because we aren't ready to plan the work. We need to prepare, do some more discovery, and examine some other technical options."

Instead of plowing forward, Margot schedules a meeting with her development leaders and lets them know she expects them to focus on quality first and to move cautiously through planning. She reminds them of the cost to reburn firmware updates onto prototypes. In the process, Martin, a development manager, mentions, "If we ship demoware early, or on time with bugs, Samantha will eat us alive." They all nod their heads in agreement.

Margot slows herself down, looking to compound her returns with early planning, and her team follows.

A little pain now, or a lot of pain later. It's so obvious it's hidden. Everyone of maturity knows saving a couple pennies today will cost you a lot later in quality. This is because we are taught to delay gratification, like savings accounts and compounding returns.

Slow the Work

A second approach is to slow down the product and development team from sprinting off a cliff. Teams in this extreme, pseudo-agile-focused world over-lean toward action, causing rewrites and the loss of operating capital. Stopping, or pausing work, is always an option—yet teams feel this is impossible because of inertia. Literally, teams, especially non-coders, think it's almost obscene to stop development. Yet in sports, time-outs are built into the rules of the game. A time-out is just a pause of gameplay to review what is not working. Of course, non-coders don't like to pause—as they only succeed when others work yet are not people managers, and when you only benefit from the work going forever, if work stops, they stop—and they think they are failing. In this scenario, push the team (not just yourself) toward planning, analysis, and logical sequencing.

Moving fast for the sake of moving fast won't end well unless you are a startup and trying to make enough money to keep operating next month. In this case, it's worthwhile to write as much code as quickly as possible to ship as soon as possible. But this book isn't written for those situations. We are dealing with quality concerns on existing products, like what the great majority of people work on day to day in their careers—software that runs businesses, large systems, and ultimately, our civilization.

Instead, the focus must be on careful planning, deliberate discovery, and a thoughtful approach to technical decisions. It's not just about code velocity, but about cultivating a culture where quality and long-term reliability outweigh the urge for immediate results. When teams slow down and invest in understanding requirements and examining technical alternatives, they lay the foundation for sustainable progress. This is especially important in environments where the complexity of code structure and business abstractions can create hidden pitfalls.

Developers and product managers alike benefit from pausing to align priorities, ensuring that each new feature is not just rapidly delivered but also robustly designed to fit into the intricate systems that run organizations. By embracing this disciplined approach, teams avoid the costly cycle of rushed releases and frantic rewrites and instead create software that stands the test of time, supporting the evolving needs of modern enterprises.

I had the opportunity to listen to renowned author and practitioner Kent Beck discuss some thought-provoking topics at a conference in 2024. Kent was there to give a keynote while promoting his latest book, *Tidy First* (Oreilly 2024), and explained some of his big ideas around why designing and delivering software is so hard.

The diagram in figure 4.1 below is Mr. Beck's—and it's logic is quite satisfying.

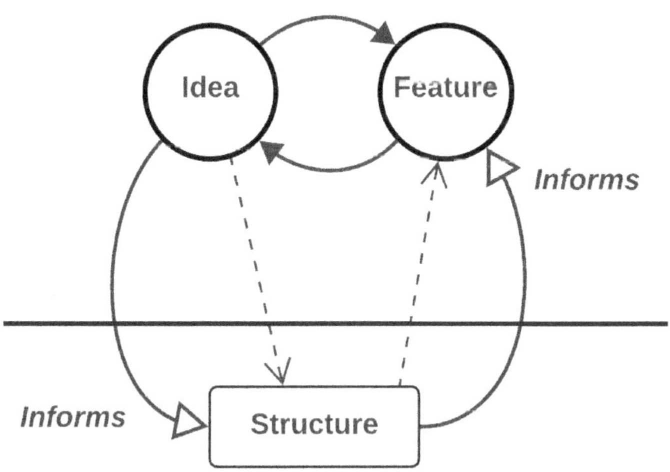

Figure 4.1 – Beck's Simplicity

When a team starts working on a new idea, their intention is to build a feature from the idea. And that idea has requirements. No one has all the requirements, least of all the product manager or the subject matter expert. No, the developer doesn't know all the requirements either—but they know something the other two do not: the structure of the code. The structure of the code is so much more important than anyone talks about because most people don't know that it matters. And for those to whom it does matter, the coders, it's all they talk about—but only amongst themselves. Imagine walking into a room where you speak English, but tables of people only speak Spanish. The folks at the table do not all stop to decipher how to communicate with you—they keep talking. Yes, the coders never stop this discussion, out loud, in forums, in meetings, online, in email, and in the comments and changes to the code base over time. It's like a long dance around a ballroom—left, right, forward, forward, right, left, left, forward, and the dance goes on.

Non-coders treat the code like magic during estimation meetings—why is one feature twenty days when another is two days and yet another is two years? Because, as discussed earlier, the structure of the code and the model that developers can only hold partially in their heads. They believe what makes code complex is that it's computer code. No! Computer code is often quite straightforward.

```
while(x is true)
{
        i = i+1;
        log(i);
}
```

This is not complex—just like learning Spanish words as an English speaker is not complex. It becomes complex as we start imposing rules upon the language, conjugating, and communicating complex thoughts. Otherwise, *hola* and *hello* are rather pedestrian terms. Software becomes complex as we add rules, integrate systems, and build software abstractions to model business. Software is all abstractions, which is the predominant reason that the structure of the code is the driving reason for its consequence to ideas and features. Even simple ideas, like a to-do list, don't model the real world as non-coders think they may. When humans think of a to-do list, they may imagine a piece of paper with five lines and a checkbox next to each one. When done, check it off. But that's not enough to build a workable to-do application for users—they always want more. Would you buy a to-do application, or download it for free where you can enter a to-do, never edit it, check it done once, and never undo the completion? Of course not—that app would be awful. Either way, that's version one.

```
ToDo todoOne = new ToDo("get the milk");
todoOne.done();
```

Figure 4.2 – Milk code

This pseudocode will accomplish two things: create a to-do object in memory with the description "get the milk," and then mark the to-do as done.

The approaches for simple things require a significant amount of brain context switching. Here are two code examples around to-dos again. The first one uses an array to manage to-dos, and the second uses a dictionary—but they do the exact same thing to the user.

```
class ToDo
{
        private List tasks = new List ();
        public void AddTask(string task)
        {
                tasks.Add(task);
        }
        public void RemoveTask(int index)
        {
                if (index >= 0 && index < tasks.Count)
                {
                        tasks.RemoveAt(index);
                }
        }
        public void ListTasks()
        {
                for (int i = 0; i < tasks.Count; i++)
                {
                        Console.WriteLine($"{i + 1}. {tasks[i]}");
                }
        }
        static void Main(string[] args)
        {
                ToDo todo = new ToDo();
                todo.AddTask("Buy groceries");
                todo.AddTask("Complete assignment");
                Console.WriteLine("Tasks:");
                todo.ListTasks();
                todo.RemoveTask(0);
                Console.WriteLine("Updated Tasks:");
                todo.ListTasks();
        }
}
```

Figure 4.3 – Milk code array

Using a dictionary:

```
class ToDo
{
	private Dictionary tasks = new Dictionary ();
	private int nextId = 1;
	public void AddTask(string task)
	{
		tasks.Add(nextId++, task);
	}
	public void RemoveTask(int id)
	{
		if (tasks.ContainsKey(id))
		{
			tasks.Remove(id);
		}
	}
	public void ListTasks()
	{
		foreach (var task in tasks)
		{
			Console.WriteLine($"{task.Key}. {task.Value}");
		}
	}
	static void Main(string[] args)
	{
		ToDo todo = new ToDo();
		todo.AddTask("Buy groceries");
		todo.AddTask("Complete assignment");
		Console.WriteLine("Tasks:");
		todo.ListTasks();
		todo.RemoveTask(1);
		Console.WriteLine("Updated Tasks:");
		todo.ListTasks();
	}
}
```

Figure 4.4 – Milk code dictionary

Now, the requirement comes to allow making the to-do "undone" when the user asks for it—and let the abstractions begin. Here are some options:

1. State management
    i. The code may hold the state of the doneness of the item internally in memory.
    ii. It may hold that same state in a database.
    iii. The code holds no state, the code is dumb, and all the state behavior is stored in a database.
2. Behavior
    i. Does the to-do have a state of done and undone?
    ii. Does another entity manage the behavior for the to-do, such as, the to-do object is dumb with some data, but a manager process attributes the to-dos "doneness" to it?
3. What happens when the user closes the app? How will it return to where they left off?

A core abstraction concern in computer science is where the behavior sits and where the state of a given instance sits. A human may be at rest sitting—their state. And they may be writing an agitated email to their boss, their behavior. In software, we have to decide where to model these concepts, and there are dozens, if not hundreds, more decisions requiring choosing just to get such a simple concept out the door. So how a developer adds the feature to undo a to-do item is highly dependent on the structure of the code. And the structure of that code cannot easily be predicated by a new developer to the team, let alone a requirements analyst or product manager overseeing the product line. A simple to-do list app may have dozens upon dozens of different implementations. Each line of code is simple—but as they string together the variances increase and the intricacy mounts, they say, "Let the user undo their to-do completion." The developer says, "Okay, that will be one day of work." And of course, the wise product managers ask, "Why?"

And the developers let them know it is because the to-dos state resides in the database, so we have to make changes to the database to allow multiple states. And that's not just a code change; it's a system change, and the rabbit hole sinks further and further until there is no light at all.

The lesson? Structure of the code matters immensely.

Yes, ideas lead to features. And yes, features often generate more ideas—and thank goodness for this, as ideas are what support our careers in the software industry. Ideas and features, features and more ideas, are the lifeblood of the business of software. But the structure of the code, more so than the code itself, is the plasma, blood cells, and platelets—everything in the blood you can't see. If I cut myself while preparing dinner—a delicious roast beef—you may see my blood and exclaim, "You're bleeding!" But, when constructing software, a coder would witness the same blood and think, "You're losing some blood cells and some valuable oxygen transportation. You should take care of that now and figure out how to avoid that next time." It's all in the details.

Combining the two actions described above, slowing yourself down and slowing down the work together creates social environments, and usually, physically technical environments that are easier to manage.

> The Management Time Money Disruption Effect: A manager can only see cost and time compression and not quality.

Reduce Cost

The goal of software design is to reduce cost. We design software so others can conceptualize it. This is because if others can't conceptualize the software through its design, they can't make changes to it. Now, software that is hard to change is bad because it's stuck. An adult who behaves like a child is said to be in arrested development, and the same happens to software that is not changeable. The industry term, which sounds more polite than arrested development, is that it lacks maintainability. Which, again, is just another way to say, "This system is really hard to change," which happens for about as many reasons as there are fish in the sea—more than we care to know. Once other developers can change the software, they can build features from ideas on top of the codebase (yes!), and because they can understand the software and make changes to it, the cost is less than if it's difficult to change the software.

Think of this simply. If it takes two hours to change a small feature for printing outputs in serif fonts versus two days, that is a more cost-effective outcome. Why? Because businesses costs run by the hour—so this feature change may take three hundred dollars for two hours of work versus nine hundred dollars for a couple days of work; hence, the good design, allowing change, reduces the costs. The reason we make changes to software as fast as possible is to sell more. Now, this idea of selling can be realized in revenue, deadline attainment, or safety critical system updates, like fly-by-wire software in planes.

The overall quality of any software system is closely linked to the quality of the software design and structure of the code.

Incentives

Sales teams are incentivized to close deals, so they make their sales numbers and fill their bonuses. This is why the tension between everyone in a company and the sales teams exist—they have to be different, because if they stop pushing, all is lost. Few products exist that don't need smart, capable, and tenacious sales associates. Alas, the sales team's incentive is different than that of the product team. A product team is looking at the market fit, competitors, a couple years down the road, and how everything fits together with today's revenue models. They aren't compensated for massive sales directly. Meanwhile, the sales team is incentivized directly—straight line, written down in front of them, and sometimes on a sales wall. It's competitive. Product management and development is not competitive—it's a team sport.

Pressure and Quality

Yeah, there is that old trite analogy that enough pressure creates diamonds, but I think that's nonsense. Usually, intense pressure creates fractures, destruction, and obliteration. In business, to keep quality high, we want to reduce pressure so that individuals make smart, coherent decisions, and all parties are incentivized.

Teams under pressure must depend on instinct. These rote patterns may not produce the outcomes for the problems in front of them, but instead create outcomes for other, hidden incentives or punishments. Here are a few examples:

1. Teams can make poor tradeoffs in code structure and requirements fulfillment to attain static schedule success.
2. Leaders may rearrange priorities of product development teams for political gain with other stakeholders.
3. QA teams, often at the bottom of the pecking order, will reduce the scope of test case execution to meet the needs of anyone above them.

So we want to reduce pressure by slowing down. When the leaders start to slow down, the leads replicate this, and eventually the product development cadence can reduce to manageable levels to measure quality. The team can control the complexity of solutions under construction and create space for themselves to manage risk and prepare for other scenarios not on their happy path user flows. This slowing down helps us move from high-risk areas where problems can spiral upward nonlinearly. In football, the best field goal kicker can still only kick about sixty yards. He can kick a twenty, thirty, forty, fifty and that elusive sixty if he's good. But no one is making a seventy-yard field goal. Thus, a football coach understands the limits. If his team has eighty yards to go for a touchdown, he's not pulling out the field goal kicker. But when we are building software teams, we forget there are any constraints at all—pull it all in. Sign up for a hundred hours of work in a forty-hour week.

Allocate time to slowly work on the code base, proactively fixing issues, so that others who want to move fast don't knock down the building. Approaching the software from this perspective is free, requires no additional investment, and will increase quality from the bottom up.

"Slow is smooth, smooth is fast." - Navy seal mantra, to take your time, be careful, and think things through before rushing forward

Going back to Boeing, that wasn't all Stan Deal, the head of Boeing's commercial airplanes division, announced during their crisis.

"We recently instructed a major supplier to hold shipments until all jobs have been completed to specification," Deal wrote in a letter to Boeing employees. He said the delay in shipment would affect the company's production schedule, but would also help improve overall quality.

"This is what we mean when we say that we will go slow to get it right," Deal said.

Simple

Ready for more Indiana Jones? Again, in *Raiders of the Lost Ark*...Indiana and Marion walk through the open-air market in Marakesh. Marion picks up a few goods, and Indiana rises up out of a crouch with another bag of supplies when four masked thugs bearing swords rush them. Indiana pushes the first one over, punches the second, and turns to the third, whom he tries to wrestle a sword from. Marion is tangled with another thug, turns away, grabs a metal can, and swings back the opposite way, slamming the intruder in the face. A second turns towards her, and she slams him with the same can. Indiana kicks one of the masked men away, turns, grabs Marion from beating a thug, and says, "Marion, get out of here!" While she is processing this information, he yells, "Duck!" and pushes her down, punching a ruffian in the face.

The two of them spin on their heels and run out the alley, all while mobs of people yell and scream over the action. Twenty yards away, a long cart with raised sides and an open back full of hay sits open. Indiana picks up Marion and tosses her into the cart, where she lands gently, bouncing on the hay. He quickly turns and pulls the whip from his belt just in time to meet more masked thugs. He cracks the whip violently at the men, once, twice, and they step back, not wanting to feel the sting. As Indiana weighs what to do next, the driver of the cart urges his horses, and they take off with Marion!

Indiana chases the cart, and another assailant throws his body into Indiana, knocking him into a pile of pots. Around the bend, Marion hops off and is chased by yet another thug, this time with no mask. She turns a corner, and grabs a steel pan that she waves at him menacingly. Slowly, the assailant pulls a knife from his cosset, and shows it to her—smiling all along, crooked teeth, vacant gaze. He laughs at her situation. Marion turns, runs, turns another corner and jumps into an open doorway. Her pursuer sees her, slows down, and walks in through the archway. Gong! Thud. His body goes down, and we see him slowly dragged into the room.

Indiana runs through a crowd, finally free of his chasers, and slows down, returning to the cart, finding it empty of Marion. Twenty yards ahead, the crowd parts, and a large, muscular man in black with a red sash steps out of the crowd. He spins a four-foot-long scimitar, glistening from the sun, and the crowd grows quiet in anticipation. The muscle-bound man smiles, confident in his strength and his swordsmanship. Indiana, exhausted and frustrated, examines the new menace, pulls his pistol from its holster at his waist, and casually shoots the man in black.

That scene had all the makings of an epic boss scene. Gallery clears out. Music crescendos. Big man in the black and red garb looks ready to rumble, acting all tough and showing off before fighting, and Indiana Jones just sighs him off and blasts him away in one second. Pure movie magic.

And simple. Just so simple. Indiana had no need to engage; he had just fought hard and knew he had more hard work ahead saving Marion. So the simplest solution was the best solution.

A Not-So-Novel Approach

When you simplify, it's not about the context or the environment you're working in—it's the problem itself. Solve the right problem. Make the problem you're solving simpler. Reduce the friction to what your goal is so the goal is easier to achieve. It's quite different from go slow to go fast—this is more like reducing a fraction so it's easier to solve.

Which fraction is easier to comprehend: 2/3 or 3,084/4,626?

There are three core strategies to boost quality while making the solution simpler.

1. Isolate and increment the software.
2. Modularize and partition parts of large systems.
3. Sequential autonomous workflow (which we'll address in chapter 6).

Below, we will break down what each of these strategies does and how it fits into the quality equation.

Isolation

Developers talk about isolating everything. This is pure science. When doing experiments in the lab, there are control variables and non-control. The non-control variables are the independent variables (that are manipulated) and the dependent variables, which are the effects under observation. So, just like a lab experiment, developers are constantly trying to control the environment to verify behavior and values. Any change to software is dangerous because of, literally, all the variables at play in a runtime stack of executing computer code.

Thus, the smart choice is to isolate. For instance, let's say we are introducing a new calculation to a financial services application. The developer could implement new calculation *c* by changing existing calculations and adding some conditional (if/then) statements. That could technically work, though if you're a developer reading this, you may be wincing right now. If so, keep reading. Or you could put the new calculation in its own class and instantiate that class as an object when required at runtime. This new class and function are tested in isolation by developers and by automation tests. Even QA team members may be able to access the code/library/service to run tests against it. It is isolated.

Think about it like this: Every normal US single family home has a circuit breaker box, or an electrical panel. This is the hub of power distribution for the home. Besides distributing power, as the conduit from outside power lines, it provides overload protection to the individual circuit. When the home was wired up, electricians made the decision about where to isolate power supplies. Each circuit is inserted into a panel, and the wiring from the locations in the home run directly to that circuit. For instance, they may have one circuit breaker for the master bedroom, one for each bathroom, three for the kitchen, etc.

This way, when your son and daughter who share a bathroom plug in a floor heater and a phone charger, and turn on a hair dryer, causing an overload, that circuit breaker will flip, stopping the power, and the rest of the house can continue on. The circuits provide the isolation, and the isolation provides safety, thus controlling risk. This way, you can turn off power to the whole home or individual locations, and the risk of fires is greatly reduced.

Isolation is the triggering factor for incrementing software as well. When we increment, large changes are avoided. Instead of ripping out an entire set of calculation libraries, we instead strangle it off (yes, there is a pattern called the strangler) such that there is less and less of the old code and more of the new code over a period of time. This reduces risk of regression failures and introduces new code safely.

Isolate new and risky things—again, it's free, and quality improves by default.

Modularize

Even the least technical among a software project team can often speak coherently about modularization in today's environment of APIs, microservices, and distributed computing. Ever since the Apple App Store appeared and took over the world, the majority of the population can understand that an app is different than their phone (the genius of the App Store deserves its own book). The phone is its own thing, even if its users don't know it's running an operating system called iOS. Pressing the App Store picture on an iPhone, tapping through the App Store, "Get"-ing an app, seeing it on the screen, then long-pressing to delete and having it exit your world is a normal occurrence.

It's not that complex a concept, akin to stacks of boxes, or how molecules are made up of other atoms. Not simple enough? Well, how about rooms in a house? They are all rooms, yet they serve different purposes. Sue can sleep in her bedroom without her mattress distressing the efficacy of the oven in the kitchen—they are separate. Never will someone turning on the water in the master bathroom make someone wet in the garage (hopefully).

Using this pattern has produced advantages to the maintenance and long-term quality of systems for generations. APIs have been all the rage the last decade, but that's just purely a business concern. Internal APIs inside companies are boring and nothing special. Connecting system A to system B inside a company is as mundane today with REST APIs as it was in the late '90s with whatever technology people chose then. It's packaging data, sending bits over a wire, and sending bits back in response—request/response, client/server, client/client, peer-to-peer—it's just bits over a wire.

Still, the general-purpose ease of use for REST APIs today is outstanding, and it should continue that way with the myriad of tooling in support and just about any developer understanding how to connect two different systems and make remote method calls.

Servers are also modularized today. No longer is a server a stand-alone piece of computing infrastructure, or even a virtual machine—they are now containerized, a direct reference to the server as a module. A container takes the required essence of a business purpose and reduces the operating system support to the level of the application running. It's best seen with technology like Kubernetes where handfuls to dozens to thousands of containers are stacked next to each other and allow hot-swapping, redundancy, deployment, and more fancy operating mechanisms than we can enumerate here. This topic, containers and Kubernetes, has dozens of books concerning it.

Encapsulation and separation of concerns is still my favorite way to introduce modularization to people because it's in the code, where everyday decisions are made that drive feature quality that has the greatest effect on outcomes. After all, deciding to take thirty microservices and run them in containers inside a cloud provider is a one-time decision that becomes a pattern for that piece of software. But it's a decision, and once made, it doesn't need additional cognitive support going forward, which is quite different than actively trying to write new features into software consistently. Encapsulation groups code behavior together so that its data is private (hidden), outside code can only call methods or touch data it's allowed to, different programmers can handle their own code while working together, and maintainability is greatly improved by providing all the features above as development continues. All in all, encapsulation isn't a thing, it's a way of constructing software through behaviors that the code created. And it's incredibly powerful—even when done poorly.

Second is the separation of concerns that is possible when code is encapsulated during feature construction. Here, a concern might be the ability to write to a database while executing financial transactions. In our example, the following actions take place:

1. Read a file
2. Put the data into memory defined as objects
3. Run some methods on the data (the calculations)
4. Store the data

Once the code gets to step four, store the data, storage is a concern. In this case, the data is stored in a database, and that activity comes with a ton of baggage: for instance, the database driver, database connections, the type of transaction to execute, authentication, and transaction completion. We do not want our financial calculation to know anything about this business, nor do we want developers specializing in quantitative calculations messing around with mundane, though vitally important, application infrastructure concerns like reading and writing to a database.

Concern A = Financial calculations

Concern B = Writing to a database

A diverse, multi-talented team shouldn't have everyone doing everything all the time. There may be thousands of different calculations to create, improve or update annually. But with the database, like the Kubernetes examples, you set it and forget it. Separating concern A and concern B allows these teams to operate independently from each other's existence. It's one of the most beautiful abstractions in software and a key underlying concept of *Quality Is Free*.

Mixing concerns is a major cause of defects and quality degradation in software. It's like crossing the streams in *Ghostbusters*...nothing good can come of it, and it's not necessary. Nothing positive happens from making software into soup when it should be three distinct foods on a plate. It's mixing business logic with mundane application infrastructure code that promotes all of these nasty outcomes:

- Hard to debug
- Hard to read
- Hard to change

Stephanie wants to make a change to the business logic but accidentally updates a file that controls the database authentication. These worlds should never connect. Controlling randomness and emergent, unintentional behavior is not expensive, and it does not require new tools or new staff.

One last example of modularity in software is the micro-kernel architecture pattern.

The micro-kernel architecture pattern is commonly used in software development for creating systems requiring extreme flexibility and linear development workstreams. It organizes the system into a core (kernel) and multiple surrounding modules that interact with the core. It's easy to think about this pattern as a layered onion. At the center is the kernel, and each surrounding layer consists of modules, components, and user space functionality. A financial transaction system may have core calculations, like the NAV (net asset value) to describe the value of an investment fund, like a mutual fund, as seen in figure 4.5. It's calculated by subtracting the fund's liabilities from its assets and then dividing the result by the number of outstanding shares. NAV is calculated at the end of each trading day and is the per-share value of the fund. All other calculations of the fund are then based on the NAV—like the NAV return, yield, and expense ratio. Therefore, the core of the calculation stack for funds is the NAV, and the surrounding layers and isolated calculations are the calculations depending on NAV.

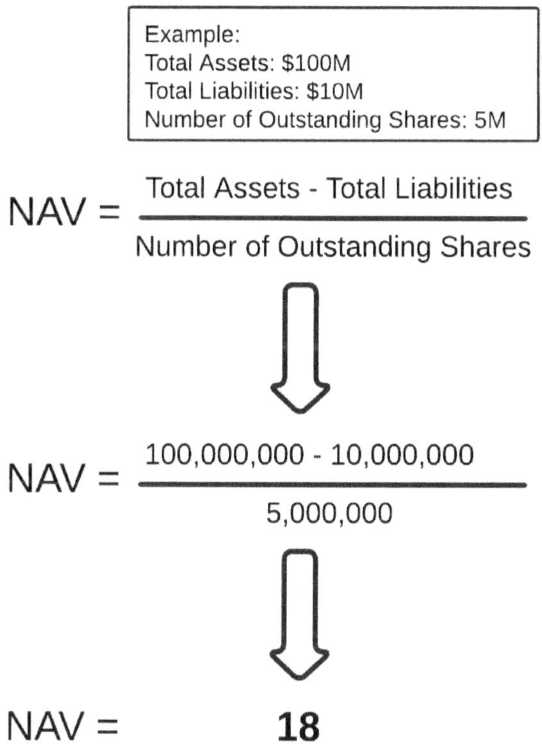

Figure 4.5 – NAV Pricing Example

Summary

Like Marion and Indiana, overcommunicating would couple them together and thus weaken their defense against the assault. In their case, it was important that one of them looked left while one looks right. That's how they conquered their dire circumstances and came away uninjured.

As you've read, slowing down when risk lurks in the way is important. And then you saw how critical it is to keep things simple. Now, combining these practices is what yields the massive results. After all, if you could avert a project disaster and possibly millions of dollars of repercussions by planning some more—wouldn't you do it? Imagine if you had a superpower to have hindsight. That's what this is—slow and simple. It's so boring, it's brilliant.

Takeaway

Complicated things are different than complex. Software projects deal with complexity because there are many interrelated processes and services producing unpredictability. But each piece isn't usually that complicated.

Slow down

- Slow yourself down
- Slow the work down
- Manage incentives

Simple

- Isolate things that change
- Modularize to reduce complications
- Manage bigger concerns sitting above the code

Next, we'll take a look at the industry machinations generating unneeded hype that will try to slow down your progress.

5 – Hype Machinery

In 2016, the Pokémon Go app craze took not just the US but the world by storm! Millions of kids and adults turned into hunters of friendly virtual monsters called Pokémon. The game company Niantic launched the augmented reality mobile game in July, leading to players wandering streets, parks, and even sometimes across private property to catch these Pokémon using their smartphones.

Within weeks of launch, Pokémon Go was a global movement and phenomenon the likes of which no one had seen before. People were glued to their phones, chasing the virtual characters Charizard, Pikachu, and Lechonk across playgrounds, parking lots, and town squares. Busineses got in on the action too—offering discounts for Pokemon Go players on the move. The fad was in full effect. But a downside was imminent—and once it came, the mood started to change considerably. People walked into traffic, were caught trespassing on private property, or suffered addiction to their screens and games, unable to stop. Reportedly, a teen in Wyoming found a dead body while searching for a water Pokemon near a river. Norway's prime minister, Erna Solberg, was documented playing the game in both professional and personal settings—multiple times in parliament and famously once before a meeting with United States president Donald Trump in 2016.

By 2017, the Pokémon Go fad was fading. The initial intense frenzy wasn't sustainable, with server errors, repetitive gameplay, and player exhaustion setting in. Daily active users dropped significantly, but the game didn't disappear altogether, and today it still retains a player base. More importantly, that crazy mobile game left a mark: It popularized augmented reality gaming, paving the way for similar apps and proving that technology could blend the digital and physical worlds in meaningful ways.

Pokémon Go ended up being more than just a game, more than a fad—it was a whirlwind of innovation, community, and chaos that reshaped how we think about mobile games. Additionally, the game fad surged interaction and interest in Pokémon products, licensing, and their trading cards. Pre-Pokemon Go, the company averaged around $4 billion to $5 billion in annual revenue and by 2022 generated $11.6 billion with $320 million as profit. Some may only know the game—but that brand and the company behind it have more than doubled their revenue.

Handling fads in life, or an industry like technology, is like exposure therapy—the more you deal with them, the more flexible you'll be when the next set of nonsense knocks at the door. See, technical executives want everyone to take them seriously, even though the advice changes annually. If your financial advisor changed your investment strategy every fourteen months, would you keep them? Well, in tech, that's how it works out (mostly); there are some fundamentals that stay, but we are battered by the waves of fads consistently.

Understanding the characteristics of software systems will allow you to make empirical judgements on the perceived quality of a given system.

No One Is Coming to Save You

If you can run a forty-yard dash in 4.3 seconds and leap eleven feet off the ground, you could have a contract in the NFL for $5 million a year, right? Heck, $10 million—those are some amazing stats! Well, if you can produce zero defects, you can make five or ten million more a year too. Seriously, if you took the software you're working on that, say, generates $20 million annually, and can show the market it is without defect, customers will exit their other contracts and get on board. It's like buying a car that never needs maintenance; you'd want that car.

Well, why aren't you doing it?

Because it's just not possible.

No one can jump eleven feet in the air, and no one can produce zero defect software. It's just a pipedream that most in this industry have given up on. Don't go for zero defects. Trust me, your QA team will make up a defect before admitting that none exist.

Trust me, your QA team will make up a defect before admitting none exist.

The Shift Left Fad

Though some fads may yield some positive long-term outcomes, most are just a waste of money. Like the pet rock. Or painting your entire room grey.

Tech fads—now these are dangerous. These fads are dressed up as trends, but we know what they are, and it's not necessary to enumerate the many rise-and-fall technologies and techniques over the years. There is nothing wrong with new ideas—it's the marketing and socialization of them as dogma where things become iffy.

Lately, it's fashionable to promote the concept of moving software delivery and operations work from the right side of the equation to the left. The generally accepted term for this idea is "shift left." It's all the rage.

Here are some examples:

1. Are you having problems with the quality of a software release? Well, then take your testing approach and shift it left.
2. Did your last security audit have more red lines then you're comfortable with? We have a solution—take the security analysis and work and shift it left.
3. How about every last detail of building out some cloud or datacenter infrastructure for your project? Shift left!

This leads to a few challenges:

1. A major narrative fallacy
2. Time compression
3. The same timelines, but with a different set of expectations
4. Poor results everywhere (now development can't get started, and once they are started the load has gone up)

There is one thing the Shift Left Gang ignores—business results. When the purpose of selling software is to sell said software to software developers, it doesn't matter if it improves outcomes. It only matters that it fulfills the expectation set forth in that sales cycle. This is like pricing art: If it brings you joy, isn't it worth five thousand to you or twenty thousand to someone with deeper pockets?

For instance, imagine you buy a new dishwasher. It cleans the dishes (as advertised), but it gunks up your drain lines, requiring monthly cleaning. The dishwasher salesman sold you a device that gets your dishes sparkling clean. It's not their problem if the drain lines back up because they can't filter out waste from the drain.

Such is the myth of shifting left. Look at who talks about it—it's not software developers! It's everyone else who wants to criticize and tell software developers what to do. You see, all functions want to control software, because, well, they aren't in software and it's hard for some teams not to see how the sausage is made.

Therefore, application development consultancies want to sell you "services" to "learn" how to shift left. Security software companies want to sell you software that will inject processes into development. And the big analysis companies (not to be named here) need to sell you more market research and analysis, which means they need new things to sell, and when all you sell is words, you need new words and themes. The same goes for the surrounding functions—they are essentially non-functional requirements which, in today's culture, insist on being functional requirements. But it's not so.

The surface area of attack on a web application is not the same as "the application will save the user's last transaction so they can retrieve it later for reporting."

Functional = Business Requirements

Everything Else = Non-Functional Requirements

The truth, if anyone cares to share it, is that non-functional requirements in most cases are non-requirements, meaning they don't exist. Getting a product out to market, to make revenue, to test the market's appetite, doesn't require a "sense of ownership" over infrastructure, security, or anything else. It requires everyone to do their jobs, but it doesn't mean that the software developer must be an expert now at QA, automation testing, product analysis, cloud operations, build pipelines, penetration testing, and 1,001 security aspects. All the other functions forget, regularly, that software developers are already experts at many technologies and domains, with a very short, sample outline in table 4.1 below.

1. The subject matter they are working in
2. A range of programming languages
3. All the technologies to execute #1 and #2 above

Table 5.1 – Things Programmers Already Know

Languages	*1. C#* *2. Java* *3. Html* *4. JavaScript* *5. SQL* *6. Python* *7. Etc.*

Computer Paradigms	1.	*Deploying into containers*
	2.	*Deploying serverless*
	3.	*Developing locally, developing remotely*
	4.	*Source control build and git*

The developer can't also be a cloud expert, QA expert, networking expert, and security expert.

With every function around the actual software development of business features wanting to shift left directly into development, we end up with nothing shifting because a hundred units of work over a given timeline is still a hundred units if you try to do it all at once or over a period of time. It's a major fallacy. A hundred units is a hundred units. And not every function for an entire tool chain of non-functional requirements can be done at once.

Therefore, shift left (testing) is not helpful for every project. It depends on the context, the scope, the team, and the customer. Sometimes, it may be more beneficial to have a balanced approach, where testing is performed at different stages of the development cycle according to the needs and risks of each project. This way, we can ensure that testing is efficient, effective, and aligned with the business objectives.

Methodologies

Patterns to manage software projects have always been called methodologies. I assume this academic term was preferred to approach technology strategy because it sounded more intimidating. It's a shame though, because it's spurred debates in areas that usually didn't require such intense debate. Let's start our review over the last twenty-five years with the one mega, dominating methodology in the room which takes first place by a mile—all while denying being a methodology—Agile!

1. Agile

Agile, established in 2001 with the Agile Manifesto, changed software development by emphasizing flexibility, collaboration, and iterative progress over linear processes like Waterfall. They had good reason, watching software failures repeatedly, and experiencing the unenviable feeling of wasting their lives. Created by seventeen industry leaders (on a mountain somewhere), it focuses on four values: individuals and interactions, working software, customer collaboration, and responding to change. Agile allows teams to deliver small, functional increments, adapting to changing requirements. It has influenced various industries, contributing to frameworks such as Scrum and Kanban. However, Agile's flexibility can lead to scope expansion, inadequate documentation, and challenges in large-scale projects.

Despite these issues, Agile's adaptability is fundamental in dynamic development environments, necessitating disciplined execution. The problem is that no one is disciplined. Therefore, the coaches and proponents of these "not-a-process" processes insist on all kinds of interesting "ceremonies" like daily stand-ups and chit-chatting incessantly with each other about tasks that no one can assist with, because they are, well, just work. And if everyone could help everyone with their work, no one would get their work done. It's a nasty little spiral.

2. Scrum

Scrum, an Agile framework developed in the 1990s by Jeff Sutherland and Ken Schwaber, became notable in the 2000s for its structured yet adaptable approach. It organizes work into two-to-four-week sprints, with specific roles (Scrum Master, Product Owner, Development Team) and ceremonies, including daily stand-ups and sprint reviews. Scrum's focus on iterative delivery and transparency enhances team productivity and alignment with customer requirements. While effective for small-to-medium teams, scaling Scrum can be challenging due to coordination overhead. Potential issues include excessive ceremony reliance or misaligned priorities if the

Product Owner lacks clarity. Scrum's widespread use is due to early 2000s confusion where all Agile become Scrum, and Scrum was therefore Agile.

This is a framework outlined with more dogma and struggle sessions than anything else on the list. Its most frequent use is either (1) a way to create faux predictability over productivity, or (2) to create a wacky, upside-down organization where tenured engineers take orders from twenty-year-olds who can't program. The majority of the Agile coaching industry is founded around Scrum, or SAFe (below), where the coaches will often answer criticism of their Agile "recipes" with accusations that the one questioning is not educated enough, or not using the recipe well enough, or just needs some "re-education." Kind of scary? And it doesn't sound like it has anything to do with healthy teams, software, or the making of money.

It's demoralizing to ask a seasoned professional to play games, like planning poker. And if you're not familiar with this, please ask your favorite AI assistant or search engine about it.

"Doublethink means the power of holding two contradictory beliefs in one's mind simultaneously and accepting both of them." — **George Orwell, *1984***

3. DevOps

Emerging around 2009, DevOps combined software development and IT operations to speed up delivery and improve quality. Promoted by figures like Patrick Debois, it focuses on automation, continuous integration/deployment (CI/CD), and cross-team collaboration. Tools such as Jenkins, Docker, and Kubernetes are central to DevOps, enabling rapid and reliable releases. By 2020, 83 percent of organizations reported adopting DevOps practices, according to Atlassian. However, DevOps requires significant cultural changes, as siloed teams may resist transformation, and automation involves initial investments. Companies like Amazon deploy code frequently due to DevOps, though poor implementation can cause burnout or security issues.

DevOps isn't really a software methodology, but everyone thinks it is. Note how IT is in the definition, which, in the framework of this book, makes the topic quite interesting. See the outstanding book, *The DevOps Handbook,* by Gene Kim et al.

4. Kanban

Kanban, adapted for software development in the 2010s from Toyota's manufacturing system, employs visual boards to manage workflows and limit work-in-progress (WIP). Popularized by David J. Anderson, it supports continuous delivery without fixed iterations, suitable for teams handling unpredictable tasks. Digital Kanban boards track tasks through stages like "To Do," "In Progress," and "Done." Kanban's simplicity improves transparency and efficiency, but it lacks Scrum's defined roles, which can complicate larger projects. Overloaded boards or neglected WIP limits reduce effectiveness. Kanban's flexibility is beneficial for maintenance-heavy or creative teams.

Kanban—it's great for working on defects or a three-person team.

5. Scaled Agile Framework (SAFe)

Introduced in 2011 by Dean Leffingwell, the Scaled Agile Framework (SAFe) extends Agile principles to large enterprises, addressing coordination challenges among multiple teams. SAFe organizes work into Agile Release Trains (ARTs), guiding teams to deliver "value" every eight to twelve weeks. It includes roles like Release Train Engineer and practices like Program Increment (PI) planning. By 2023, 37 percent of large organizations used SAFe, according to Scaled Agile Inc. SAFe aligns complex projects but is sometimes seen as overly prescriptive, potentially leading to bureaucracy. Its structured approach is suitable for sectors like finance or aerospace, requiring substantial training and cultural adoption to maintain team autonomy. Which means, in all, SAFe is the recreation of frameworks from the '80s and '90s, except now with Agile in the name. I'm sure it has good uses when regulation or safety criticality is at the top of the list, but at that point, just use an older methodology that produces a better paper trail.

All of these methodologies are just since the year 2000, and trust me, a lot happened before then. Let's look at some of the crowd favorites pre-2000.

More Methods of Fun-ology

1. Waterfall

The Waterfall model, introduced by Winston Royce in 1970 and popularized in the 1980s, is a linear approach dividing development into distinct phases: requirements, design, implementation, testing, deployment, and maintenance. It emphasizes thorough documentation and planning but struggles with changing requirements. This approach was born out of the Industrial Age, drawing on construction and manufacturing where there weren't the ideas of iteration or fail fast, because you can't half-build a bridge. And one other thing—everyone misunderstands Waterfall!

People who weren't around in the '90s have only a vague impression of what Waterfall was. Nowadays, we often hear teams say any work that requires planning and analysis is Waterfall. Nope. Waterfall was extremely rigid. One you moved from one phase, like design, to the next, like implementation/coding, going back is impossible. Did you make a mistake? Did the client want a four-bedroom house and you're building a four-bedroom tent? Tough luck.

However, this should make you feel warm and fuzzy versus generating that sense of loathing: Waterfall is still used! Industries like aerospace, or nuclear reactors, cannot just be undone. And, to put a bow on this greatly misunderstood, great-grandfather of all methodologies—Mr. Royce didn't even call this process Waterfall, and he himself warned of its limitations with phases. Sometimes you just can't win.

2. Spiral

Developed by Barry Boehm in 1986, the Spiral model combines iterative development with risk management. It consists of four phases—planning, risk analysis, engineering, and evaluation—and repeats until project completion. Ideal for complex projects but has high overhead due to its focus on risk assessment.

3. Rapid Application Development (RAD)

Introduced by James Martin in 1991, RAD prioritizes speed and flexibility through iterative prototyping, user feedback, and minimal planning. Effective for projects with tight deadlines but can result in poorly structured code and struggles with large-scale projects. In many ways, this was the precursor to Agile, often generating chaos.

4. Rational Unified Process (RUP)

Created by Rational Software in the 1990s, RUP blends iterative and disciplined development across four phases—inception, elaboration, construction, and transition. It requires significant training and tooling, suitable for large, complex projects but often seen as bureaucratic. RUP was marketed hard, but adoption was impossible in most cases because of the need for extreme discipline and the lacking ROI cases to support the effort.

5. Feature-Driven Development (FDD)

Introduced by Jeff De Luca and Peter Coad in 1997, FDD focuses on delivering client-valued features through five processes: develop a model, build a feature list, plan by feature, design by feature, and build by feature. Effective for large teams with clear ownership but may not suit highly volatile requirements because feature coupling (where changing feature A breaks feature B) is inherently expensive to change.

Wrapping Up on Methodologies

Picking on Agile is like the proverbial saying, beware when poking the bear. It's easy to poke at Agile a lot for good reason: It's become more of an industry driven by non-technical professionals telling technical professionals what to do. It's also antiquated. When those good folks were on the mountain writing their opinion on software development practices, we barely had email, there wasn't Git for distributed source control, Linux hadn't taken off, we didn't have powerful work item management tools (like Jira or Microsoft Boards), software development insight metric tooling, or most importantly, continuous integration systems. Build platforms likes Jenkins, Microsoft ADO Pipelines, or GitHub Actions greatly reduce the need for conversation and coordination or even sprint reviews because the focus shifts to productivity. Last, the practice of User Experience design (UX) is completely different than the year 2000, where tools like Figma or Miro allow absurdly rapid UX prototyping and feedback generation removing developers from that workflow entirely (in a good way).

What is most critical, and where Agile assisted, is suggesting and attempting to template the importance and emphasis on collaboration and continuous improvement. I never said Agile is evil—just misused long after its inherent usefulness.

Measuring Those Quality Metrics…Ha!

Times change, so the way we measure quality follows suit. We keep inventing new ways to measure quality and introduce more software into the world, and people are just as frustrated. As mentioned earlier in the book, the industry moves from one set of metrics that are persecuted for being antithetically problematic in usefulness before repeating the cycle with the new metric du jour.

In the golden ages of software development, managers would measure the LOC (lines of code) written per developer as the defining metric of productivity and, therefore, the worth of a given programmer (they weren't developers yet). Then the high-humility, high-hubris Agile folks came around, and the marketplace extracted so many measurements and practices that they became useless: velocity, cycle time, lead time, code coverage, cumulative flow, and burndown. It was a virtual, overwhelming succession of measurements all at once. But, like so many areas of life, many measurements mean little unless the improvement of a given number yields business results.

And as mentioned in chapter one, lately, everyone's favorite measurement is DORA, deployment frequency, mean lead time, mean time to recovery, change failure rate, and reliability. Another thoughtful piece from Google engineering, where they clearly invest a lot of time in documenting their internal processes for the industry—even if it can sometimes feel a bit challenging for teams to measure against.

Yet, somehow, we put rockets into space, put men on the moon, and operate automated nuclear facilities without any of these metrics.

Craftsmanship

The craftsmanship anti-pattern states that code must follow a prescriptive, artistic, individualistic style. It looks at software not as an engineering endeavor to be optimized, but instead as something like artisan cheese—small craft, unique and special. And, at this point, it is most likely intellectually broken, with even modest AI models producing high-quality code.

The anti-pattern shows up most often at the start of projects. So be on the lookout for this problem when projects are booting up and teams are trying to get their first few rounds of code committed.

A few years ago, my friend Susan started a vegan bakery but later wished she hadn't. Everyone around her loved the recipes she invented, the creative ingredients she sourced, and the delicious outcomes from her work. She baked breads, scones, muffins, and cookies that anyone who enjoyed even the most decadent of desserts wanted to eat.

Her friends encouraged her to open a storefront and take her vegan baking to the masses.

Quickly, she realized the time and expense of scaling her baking. It became difficult to source her quality ingredients, deal with a range of procurement costs, and, most demotivating—trying to bake her goods en masse through large commercial ovens. The results were not the same as her origin story. And even though she sold enough bakery items to cover her costs, the joy was gone. What once was Susan's craft became just commercial baking.

And in the process, since she was holding on so tight to the original techniques and recipes, she lost the chance to grow as a baker through larger-scale techniques that could have yielded more goods, more variety, and brought more people to her storefront.

Developers are encouraged to be craftsman all the time nowadays through outdated and old mode patterns—and it's detrimental. What happened to Susan happens to developers. They become enamored with their small, local, workflows and changes and can't scale to be part of a productive team. They may massage their classes and functions into subjectively uniquely opulent and efficient parameters, but they miss deadlines and overall objectives.

Loving your craft is not a problem. Doing your best work possible is not a problem. Considering your programming a craft is not a problem. It's the worship, the deification of craft above all else, that's the problem.

When you insist on craftsmanship, you are setting implicit priorities that are often antithetical to your business or outcomes. It's not just the production of revenue—where is the value for the world in handcrafting code for health care equipment? Beauty is not function. Quality is beauty.

It's absurd. Quality isn't something to insist on. It's something to do. It's like saying "We normally build total horse manure, but now we are artisans." Saying what you are doing is craft, while another developer is not, is obtuse. Apple factories manufacturing and shipping thousands of iPhones daily is a scaled operation. But it is just as amazing, and craft-worthy, as someone attempting to assemble handmade leather cases for those iPhones.

AI, Vibe, Agents

And now with AI generative code models, almost overnight, craftsmanship was wiped out in favor of agentic massive output programming using large language models. This is occurring so rapidly this is all we'll say on the topic here.

Class Is in Session for Those Who Believe Good Enough Is Actually Enough

Building software products seemed easy—just a great idea and quick sprints. But reality is different. Struggling with developers and managers, you face resistance toward your goals. Frustratingly, recent sprints produced software that lacks the promised value. What's next?

The Lesson – Engineering Is Its Own Thing

Reading product development articles online may lead to the conclusion "product development" is one big family. This may be true for startups or small companies, maybe even small teams. But it's not accurate for the enterprise. Engineering isn't just one of the six parts pictured below in figure 5.1 below.

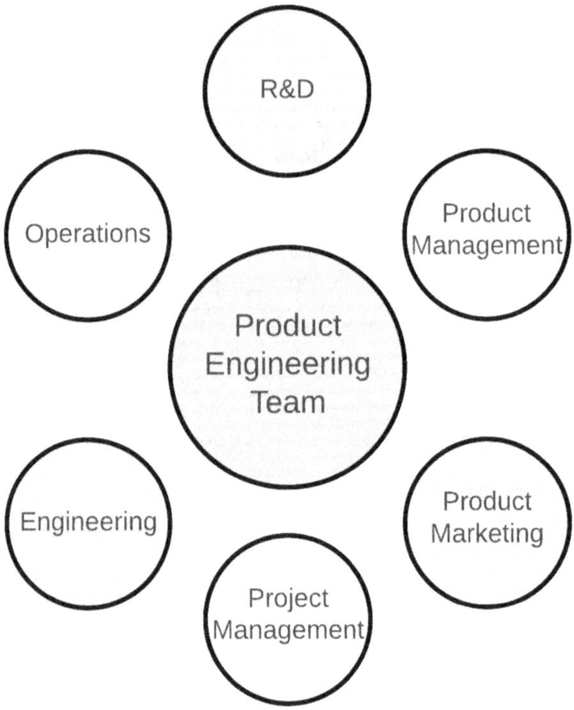

Figure 5.1 – Product Engineering Team

While product development encompasses various components, engineering stands apart with its multifaceted roles, encompassing operations, development, project management, and software development. This distinct identity of engineering shapes the backbone of technological advancements and is often considered the nucleus of innovation within a company.

These diagrams, like above, really confuse things. Engineering is the hardest group to create, the most expensive to fund, and often the purpose of the company. This is why we have so many tech founders: because tech creates tech.

Consider this analogy. Tyrel, the architect, designs a new office tower in downtown Miami named the Pinnacle. The building aims to attract commercial clients into the central business district due to its high-ceilinged design, shared common spaces, three cafeterias, and large auditorium. Tyrel's designs are distinct, and the investors in the property are optimistic about offering something different in the competitive Miami market.

Kathy runs construction engineering for the Pinnacle, and she and her team have reviewed the architectural plans hundreds of times as they plan the new build. They have a plan that provides stability in the structure, has predictability in the timeline, manages risk (for safety and cost), and achieves the goals of the investors and the architect.

After the initial dig out comes the first concrete pour. The execution of this pour is critical to the stability of the building and all the work that comes next. It's a non-trivial, non-repeatable, and unmovable task. And it's massively time consuming.

Once this pour is in place, the concrete structures start, framing the tower from the ground up. After that, Kathy's team works on multiple floors at once, using the trades and specialties—framing, electrical, engineering (load), plumbing, and inspections.

This isn't what Tyrel wants. Tyrel is expecting finished floors as he goes. He asks Kathy about his expectation, and she tells him the construction plan again. Okay, he says, he can make do.

"But Kathy, what about the auditorium? I told the investors we'd have that ready to tour in the next two months. Can you please prioritize the auditorium?"

"What?" Kathy replies.

"The auditorium. On the 33rd floor. Can you please make that a priority for the crew?"

Kathy looks confused, and this worries Tyrel.

"Kathy, this isn't a problem, is it?"

"Tyrel, yes, it's a problem. That's not the plan. And we can't just jump thirty floors to the auditorium. That will introduce a tremendous amount of risk."

"…"

"Okay? Do we understand each other? I want you to be comfortable," asks Kathy.

Tyrel pauses again. "What say do I have in the order of construction?"

"None. Unless the investors are willing to sell only half a building, or just an auditorium." She pauses. "But the city zoning and safety won't allow it anyway." Kathy shares her last sentence with as much compassion and patience as she has. It's clear that Tyrel hasn't been near the construction of a project this large before.

"Kathy, what do I tell the investors? I promised them that auditorium early in construction."

Kathy replies, "Don't worry. We're still in this together. Let's go talk to them."

Now, software is not an office tower, as software is ten times more flexible than real world construction. But with that flexibility, it can become infinitely more complex than an office tower. Most software follows the hidden path of all software: "Get stuff, show stuff, do stuff." Software of a non-trivial nature has many requirements that aren't in product feature roadmaps, like security, compliance, governance, performance, reliability, data location, etc.

So what happens in software projects when the request for "prioritization" comes in? Stopping development on workstream A to focus on workstream B is expensive. It's expensive to stop work and expensive to start work. Software can be broken down into more iterations, yes, but the idea of the prioritization factory is only possible in these cases:

1. Existing software systems
2. Software in trivial industries (e.g., not finance, health care, government, safety, etc.)
3. A business focused on short term gains

Myriads of reasons exist to pump features out nonstop at the expense of the health regarding the underlying software platform. But it comes at a cost and is unreasonable in most situations.

Concluding the Office Tower

The architect told people they would have an auditorium to show prospects by the first quarter of construction. Engineering never agreed to that.

The constructions plans include even more things than were expected. The electricians, masons, the interior designer…the architect has not yet realized he's no longer in control, and this illusion of control will continue causing problems for this project.

Value Streams and Post-Agile

You're living in Irving, Texas, excited for what's to come with the Dallas Cowboys entering the playoffs. "What a year," your neighbor comments to you over the brown picket fence as you pull the pit-style cast-iron smoker out of the garage.

"We're going to do it. We're going all the way this year!" you reply.

But that's not what happens. Instead, Dallas fails to score in the first half and loses the game by a field goal. It's all over. The expectations were so high. The fervor of the community full of optimism and excitement. Even dogs going for their afternoon walks wagged their tail with just that something extra as the season progressed.

Still. They lost. And, as per usual in sports, you win it all, or you win nothing and lose it all.

Part of finding success is measuring against the truth.

This is what the Agile product development and product management communities do to themselves, every day—they set false expectations for teams and the industry. There is a constant "refocus" on moving teams via organization to one of these paradigms:

1) Feature-based

2) Component-based

3) Value stream

Early Agile attacked component-based teams with vigor, and often for good reason. This setup did create internal, non-trivially vertical silos. Silos, often a useful structure, have also been cancelled by practitioners. They said that feature-based teams are superior, and again, for good reason. Feature teams allowed more focus on goals, fewer handoffs, more team resiliency, and generally, positive outcomes. And, finally, the modern *Agilists* canceled features teams. And what for? Value streams.

Then product managers showed up. I've said it many times: Product management is a key role connecting disparate parts of the product development practice, and we build better products with this new set of roles. But this sub-sector, self-admittedly, is new. They have the same amount of learning to go through as it did to move from assembly to java—and if you didn't know, that took decades.

And now, product managers want to mix it up again. With their arrival, early Agile is flourishing, and progress has stalled. Why? Early Agile, Scrum especially, was invented before GitHub, slack, AWS, Microsoft as a Cloud company, Zoom, and the whole slew of tooling that constitutes today's software and, hence, product development organizations. Scrum is broken; it was meant for face-to-face. But this industry spawned in the early 2000s is in firm control by 2025, so people entering the field today see early Agile as state-of-the-art. It is not.

Additionally, product management dislikes hiring from their subject or fields of expertise. Which means that the "experiment, iterate, and learn" cycles take longer and longer as the problems become complex. Creating a new alternative investment vehicle isn't accomplished by a career product manager with no subject matter expertise. The time it will take for them to even find the "problem" to perform discovery on would excise the time allotted in the market for that movement.

"When the time for action has come, the time for preparation is over."

Today, Agile and product management practitioners like to refer to a couple of interesting case studies around value stream deliveries. First (of course) is Netflix, and second is Facebook. Besides the fact that these companies are the exception to the rule (massive tech organizations acting as disruptors or first movers), their cases are selected with bias.

Netflix is crowned the king of value-based, iterative, Agile, continuous value to customers. Therefore, it's easy to think that some product managers and Scrum teams are just iterating on ideas nonstop. Well, maybe they are. But what is behinds this massive organization? I'll tell you—technology and component teams. Netflix invested into infrastructure and custom software on a scale that the world had never seen. This non-value-stream, non-product, manager-based innovation laid the foundation for the second and third generation of Netflix teams to build their feature sets. Again, it's a massive investment into core technology that made Netflix, Netflix.

Let's name just a few:

Asgard: A web-based tool for managing AWS cloud deployments and infrastructure. It simplifies scaling and monitoring but was largely replaced by Spinnaker.

Nebula: Gradle plugins to streamline software build, test, and deployment processes. Enhances productivity with modular, standardized builds.

Hystrix: A library for fault tolerance in distributed systems, preventing cascading failures. Offers circuit-breaking and real-time monitoring.

Atlas: Netflix's telemetry platform for real-time metrics and system performance monitoring. Enables quick data analysis for cloud environments.

Simian Army: Tools like Chaos Monkey to test cloud resilience by inducing failures. Ensures systems handle disruptions reliably.

But these open-source projects and the way they embrace their open source didn't drive their stock price from X dollars to Y dollars. Technologists ignore market dynamics, pricing, bundling, marketing, and, of course, content. If a restaurant is considered great, it's because of their food, not the tools they use to make the food. But, and just as an example, the Netflix team says it's their technology (which makes them great) while ignoring their content. It's just backward.

Now let's consider Facebook—they too are championed for their iterative, product-led development cycles. Well, that's just not completely accurate. Facebook is a tech firm founded and built by technologists. The amount of technology invention required is staggering. Below are just a few examples of what they developed to allow feature advancement at their incredible pace.

React: A JavaScript library for building fast, component-based user interfaces for web and mobile apps. It simplifies UI development with a declarative approach used widely by companies like Netflix.

HHVM: An open-source virtual machine for executing PHP and Hack code, using just-in-time compilation for high performance. It powers Facebook's servers but has seen declining adoption as PHP improved.

Jest: A JavaScript testing framework focused on simplicity, ideal for React applications. It offers zero-configuration testing, snapshot features, and parallel test execution maintained by the OpenJS Foundation.

Presto: A distributed SQL query engine for fast, interactive analytics on large datasets, from gigabytes to petabytes. It's used by Facebook for querying data warehouses and is supported by AWS and Teradata.

Software development is not maturing. It's stuck now with more people buying into early Agile. More people in this industry are buying into the current state of Scrum development. And they are missing the point of return, since the majority of development activities are on existing systems and require nowhere near the amount of Agile user story creation as some teams want. The second way they are missing the point is that software development doesn't reach customers alone: systems do. Networking, security, infrastructure, partner networks, quality testing, software development, and technical planning processes do. The myopic focus on early Agile and Scrum ignores the world of technology required for even the most basic of SaaS services to work. We have to tell the truth. It's not just product managers and some software developers—it's an entire village of professionals!

Ninety-nine percent of the jobs in product management or software development are on existing systems. We are maintaining and expanding systems, and different roles will call some systems products, and then ones they don't like will be ignored and the responsibility of the technology team. Once in a while, there is a large capital infusion for a new system or a rebuild, but that's a different problem, as the industry still has high failure rates on new system builds. Which, by the way, is why Private Equity Capital Investment firms prefer to glue legacy products together instead of creating something net new.

At the end of the day, what matters is the customer and delivering functionality (you can call it value or features, it doesn't matter) to customers on a somewhat regular basis. Then, it has to be secure, stable, and fast (enough), because customers just want to use what they paid for and get the outcomes they require for their own business.

Summary

What's important: bypassing fads, project evolution, and team dynamics.

Fads will never go away. That's good, because it's just ideas and excitement, and without ideas, we would be stuck. And without excitement, good ideas would never be celebrated and shared. We also saw agility isn't the only factor that goes into software construction, let alone quality. Understanding there are options, ways to perform releases, and the ability to create self-imposed or dogmatic constraints are all ways to outperform the pack.

Takeaway

Those Pokémon Go mobile games were fun—and for some the fun never stopped. The Pokémon company grew their revenue and brand dramatically, exceeding their own expectations. Software hasn't seen a winner like that since the Agile ideas, which, by now, are also either pushed on us by consultants or held dearly like an old mobile game. There are better games to play today. And there are better ways to build software—but we needed Agile, as we needed all those other methodologies, patterns, and architectures along the way. There is no butterfly without the chrysalis.

You now see that quality can come in many forms. And that over the years, quality is captured from the process without the tools we think are "the way" today. Next, we're going to take a step back and look at how work is organized: designing projects to win.

Part 2 - Action

“Vision without action is a daydream. Action without vision is a nightmare.” – Japanese proverb

6 - Design Projects to Win

Michael Lewis, a bestselling nonfiction author, published the now infamous book *Moneyball: The Art of Winning an Unfair Game* in 2003, with the movie starring Brad Pitt following in 2011. *Moneyball* is the story of Major League Baseball's 2002 Oakland A's season. Faced with a limited budget of approximately $41 million compared to larger market teams like the New York Yankees, who spent over $125 million, the A's general manager, Billy Beane, had to find new and creative ways to compete. To do this, he and his staff employed data analytics to identify undervalued players, allowing the A's to build a competitive team despite financial constraints. This unique use of statistical analysis to decision-making and player evaluation was named sabermetrics.

Bean's approach worked. The 2002 Oakland A's achieved a twenty-game winning streak and won the American League West title. On September 4, 2002, in an intense game against the Kansas City Royals, the A's set the American League record with their twentieth consecutive win when Scott Hatteberg, a catcher with bad knees before the A's and beneficiary of sabermetrics, clobbered a walk-off home run in the bottom of the ninth inning.

Sabermetrics and the A's didn't use subjective opinion of experienced talent scouts or positional managers (e.g., first base coach). Instead, they wrapped their analysis with sets of working rules and methods. For instance, Beane prioritized on-base percentage (OBP) and slugging percentage (SLG) over stats that baseball managers used like batting average, home runs, and runs batted in (RBI). Preferring players who consistently got on base instead of traditional glory stats like high batting averages, hitting home runs, or their physical attributes did not help Beane's popularity as he transformed the Oakland A's. Traditionalists like their traditions, after all, and complained where Beane didn't replace big name home run hitters. The local sports market had a field day with Bean and the A's until they started winning.

Billy Bean changed the game of baseball forever by changing how a team is constructed. They figured out a way to extract a massive amount of output from their baseball organization by designing their team to win. We can learn a lot from Billy in the software industry by designing our projects to win. Project design is directly correlated to quality because it creates all the constraints and processes to allow quality capture.

Back in chapter 1, we discussed how much software is written by lower-cost, multi-time zone developers, using requirements as their directive. And the worst thing you can do is design and build software to requirements. If you build against the requirements, you'll get a system full of features that don't work together but meet requirements. Instead, you have to design and construct software toward the desired outcomes. Designing a project, like a baseball team, is what allows you to reach the outcomes.

Project Design

While interviewing contractors to remodel our kitchen, my wife and I realized that what set each contractor apart was their project design and management process. Some had very little to say about how the project would run. Others had glossy pages with simplified flow diagrams about how the project would run, and others referred to some web-based software we'd use together during the remodel. So, with three relatively similar remodel designs, we choose the contractor with the most practical, most timeline-aggressive, and highest risk-management procedures. Their project design won the contract.

Constructing software is much more complicated than remodeling yet another kitchen (experience), but we all need to deal with staffing, service dependencies, critical paths, and risk management. The thing is, these obstacles all rise from the system architecture, and addressing these comes down to development activities. Therefore, it's up to the technical leader to design the project, as only the technical leader understands the nuances of the work ahead. Project design is an extension, or maybe a continuation, of the system architecture. Don't try to separate them too much—the desire to decompose technology from the project management required to build the system sounds nice, but it's fruitless. Why? Again, as Kent Beck famously said, "Things that change at the same rate belong together. Things that change at different rates belong apart." Trust me, when the architecture changes, that project plan will!

Designing the project is no more than curtailing a list of options and almost countless possibilities. For instance, project design options must cover

- The fastest way to deliver the solution/product
- The least expensive way to build the software
- A safe option to meet commitments for the risk averse stakeholders
- The best combination of time, cost, and risk management

Consider a time in the future requiring you to vet a project for funding. (If you've not had to do this, be pleased.) Imagine you had one architecture, but three different project design approaches. How would the people in the room react? Indignant? Scared? Excited? These emotions are triggered when people feel cornered or pressured. Now, you put a few options for how the project can proceed, meaning you're flexible, and they're going to be flexible, and the likelihood of moving increases dramatically.

If you want to deliver the project incredibly fast, that's easy—cut all the good software development practices and just pretend to test it. To achieve the least expensive build, hire cheap labor and use free tools. To deliver the safest option, to meet minimum requirements, fight over scope nonstop, and cut and trim the software development playbook by a third.

Of course, project design and good architecture are correlated, as illustrated in figure 6.1 below. Ideally, good architecture receives a good project design, and the project receives nonlinear positive effects to delivery and quality. The middle ground is more prevalent, and that's okay, too. That is either bad architecture and good project design, or good architecture and bad project design. Either of these options can keep the project alive and moving forward, with good project design overcoming bad architecture for the short term. Over the long term, who knows what will happen? And lastly, in the pit of despair is bad architecture and bad project design; in that case, start over if you can or try to void the project—either way, all the best to you.

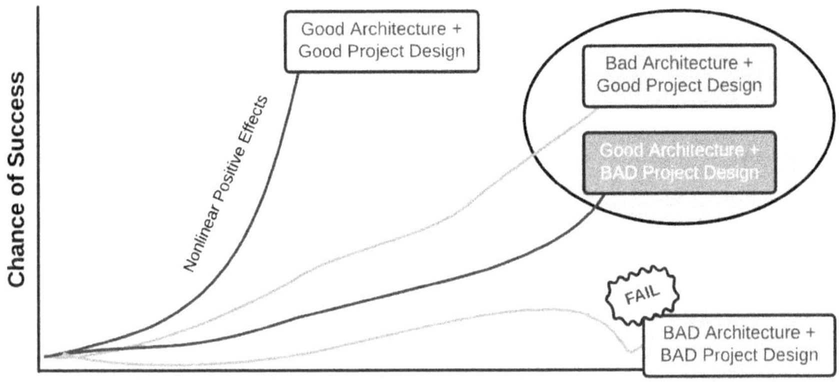

Figure 6.1 – Architecture and Project Design

Plans

It's perfectly legitimate for management teams to ask for options. Very real business reasons exist to attempt completion of Project A in three months versus nine months. In the same way, senior management may need a project to have as low a chance of failure as humanly possible, so that three-month estimate is immediately rejected as "optimistic" and they settle into thirteen months for the same work. It's okay. There is only one way to get to either of these outcomes: create a software development plan, review it, change it, review it, and commit to it.

The ultimate way to drop quality through the floor, and revenue out the door, is to fail to plan.

Overestimation and Underestimation

Overestimating work doesn't work because of Parkinson's law. If you give a developer three weeks to perform a task that should take two weeks, the following will happen: They will not work on it for two weeks, and then sit idle for a week. No, this wouldn't be so bad. What really happens: They work on it for two weeks, and then on week three, they gold plate the code. The gold plating includes adding capabilities no one needs or attempting to future-proof the solution. It gets worse sometimes, with the developer taking their shiny code and proselytizing to other team members to make changes conforming to their new machinations. In all cases, this leads to additional complexity on the task, increasing the testing footprint, reducing chances of success, and negatively impacting the overall quality profile. Basically, it makes life difficult.

When work is underestimated, teams experience as many problems as overestimation, just exuding from different perpendicular angles. Ask an engineer to complete a two-week activity in three days, and you will conclude with a low-quality, high-defect feature. The engineer must exclude best practices like design and testing, replacing those with short-term hacks like monolithic class structures and hard coding—all things a tech lead never wants to hear. And it gets worse. Instead of spending two weeks on the activity, those three allocated days turn into four to six weeks of bug finding, squashing, resolution, and then taking the feature and making yet more changes to get it production ready. So, underestimating can produce more bugs and an accumulation of technical debt. It's more nonlinear behavior that berates software engineers.

All together, we call this purgatory between over- and underestimating software the estimation paradox.

"The first law of bad management: When something isn't working, do more of it."

Overconfidence

Humans are overconfident. In Peters and Waterman's bestselling book, *In Search of Excellence*, they discuss their research into confidence. They conducted a study asking a random sample of male adults to rank themselves in their ability to get along with other people. Well, one hundred percent of the respondents ranked themselves in the top half of the population. Twenty-five percent thought they were in the top one percent. Comedically, when asked about athletic ability, one that seems far more objective to observe about yourself, sixty percent still ranked themselves in the top twenty-five percent. Only six percent of respondents thought their abilities to be below average.

Further, psychologist and behavioral economist Daniel Kahneman studied investors—a ripe population for overconfidence—and consistently found investors overestimated their ability to pick winning stocks or predict market movements. He described this as presenting confidence intervals. Conclusion: No one can predict the market, even when they say they can.

Probability of Success

Project design is meant to help us—so everything we do is meant to increase the likelihood to deliver the project's proposed outcomes as close to on time and on budget as possible. With that, estimation today is considered a vague practice—many going so far as labeling estimation dangerous and wasteful. (Imagine telling your kitchen contractor there was no need to estimate the effort or timebox the work!) Envision a project where the best-case estimates, using the best practices and subject matter experts, show about a one-year effort. Can you see that? Can this project be done in one month? Only with a miracle; otherwise, the chance is nearly zero. How about six months? No, that's half of the best-case estimate. Now we're getting closer to the original, so can this be completed in nine months? Maybe? How about ten months and five days? Yes, there is a shot of that happening. The same goes for one year and one month; it's probability of success is high. But what happens when we push further and forecast fourteen months to project completion? Well, the success actually starts heading back down! Why? Because if the real effort is landing between eleven and thirteen months, time spent working on this project after that nice little bell curve will yield more gold plating, future-proofing, and an increase in complexity in place of the desired product/system outcomes. See figure 6.2 below.

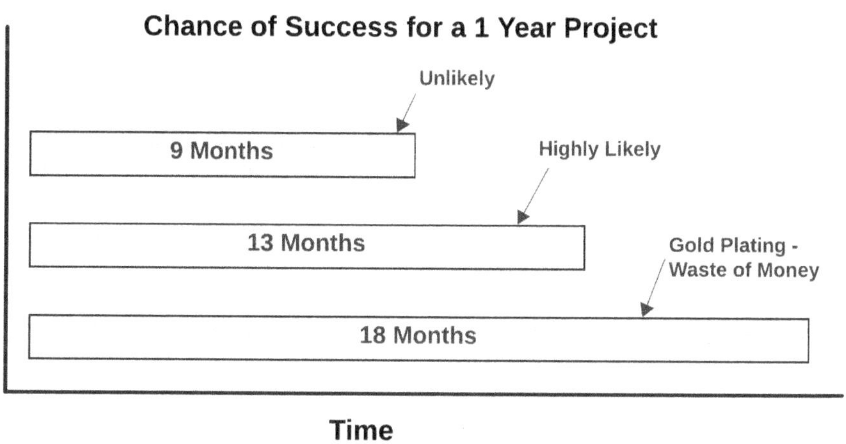

Figure 6.2 – Probability of Success

Dealing with Uncertainty

Uncertainty leads to bad estimates. And, like discussed above, the estimating activity picked up a bad reputation in the last decade—but it's not because the practice is bad; it's because of how people feel about estimating from their past experiences. Of all the activities in software project construction that become mired with cognitive dissonance, estimating earns that coveted top spot on the pedestal. Software engineers have their good faith estimates used against them in varied ways, like:

1. "You said two weeks, and that's your commitment!" from a product manager or engineering manager.
2. Upper management hearing rough draft estimates from managers and creating forecasts.
3. Sales teams projecting efforts onto development teams without requesting any estimates.
4. Agile "coaches" persuading teams to move away from estimates and only use iterative, learning-based iterations.
5. Their estimation technique inexperience leading to massively incorrect estimates.

For all the reasons above, and their negative effect on quality, you have no choice but push your teams to estimate. You can help this process along in a few ways. First, let them know estimates are estimates—they are not commitments. Separate this new-age "commitment" concept from estimating work activities. If senior engineer Carl thinks that connecting the widget to the sprocket will take four days and it takes five, who cares? If you have one hundred activities that should take four days but take five days each, that is one hundred extra days you say! Yes, it is, but that's disregarding the ten activities that took one week when they were estimated at two, with a savings of fifty estimated days.

Table 6.1 – Realities from Estimates

Feature	Quantity	Estimate	Reality	Difference	Total Diff
A	100	4 days	5 days	1 day	+100 days
B	10	2 weeks	1 week	5 days	-50 days

Do you see how subjective the estimates and their outcomes are? A project manager may escalate out of control over those. Quality isn't saving days. There isn't inherent quality in estimating "right" (which is impossible). Quality is earned through the estimation process through negation in not squeezing development into making bad choices: rushed hack jobs or gold-plated complexity.

Poor estimates aren't anywhere near as impactful as mismanaged scope, where this delta of fifty extra effort days is eventually erased with the software industry's version of balanced accounting—changing scope.

The next technique to reduce uncertainty is to frame estimates. Instead of leaving the estimator flailing in the wind, give them some guardrails using an order of magnitude, like a week, a month, or a day. That way, a group of estimators can start to think in a similar way, and it alleviates the classic problem of someone estimating in bananas and another in apples. Now, you'll have a series of estimates in a logical pattern which allows the puzzle pieces to start forming a picture.

After this, focus on the areas of the project with the following characteristics:

- The most complex and difficult to build
- The most uncertain and unknown
- Requirements that more than one developer says they just don't get

Finally, in case of emergency, here is the break-the-glass approach. Seriously, only use this formal process when estimating is feeling very wrong in your gut or the numbers are coming in far above where the business can afford it. This last step is important because quality will become expensive if the estimates become less of estimates and more of team padding or over-aggressiveness. There are a number of formal estimation processes, but the PERT method is simple enough—just plug in the values. PERT (program evaluation and review technique) takes three estimations as input: the most optimistic, the most pessimistic, and the most likely.

$E = O + 4*M + P \quad / \ 6$

1. E is the end calculation
2. O is the optimistic estimate

3. M is the likely estimate

4. P is the pessimistic estimation

Let's look at an example estimation with PERT. The team is estimating how long it will take to replace an API callback displaying erratic behavior with a message queue. Sonya is closest to this functionality, and she brings an optimistic estimate of eight days, pessimistic of twenty days, and a most likely of eleven days.

E = 8 + 4*11 + 20 / 6

So, in this case, the estimate from the PERT calculation is twelve. Use this estimate and move on.

Time and Cost

You can reduce the size of computer files (digital files) without losing essential information inside of them. This is done using algorithms which encode data efficiently, resulting in a smaller size, taking up less space in storage, and therefore being sent across the internet rapidly. Compression is what allows music and video streaming over the internet to work. There are two types of compression: first, lossless. This method maintains all original data, allowing for perfect data reconstruction after decompression. This is used for things like text, because you can't easily lose text and maintain meaning. The second type of compression is lossy. Lossy compression removes, permanently, some data to achieve size reduction. It's used for audio, video, and images where some of the fidelity of the original is acceptable.

Teams are squeezed during projects to compress total time consumed, overall costs, or both—so they have to make some tradeoffs. When teams apply lossless compression to their projects, they can spin out of control, because you can't squeeze water out of water. Here, teams can try strategies like parallel work or using better trained people.

You can also apply lossless compression to projects, which is what most projects do. What is that called? Scope reduction of course. Do less. Remove requirements. If you want to pay less for eggs by less eggs, it's straightforward and doesn't require much technique or comprehension, which on its own may prove more valuable than the time to come up with lossless solutions while preserving quality. Someone may make the academic argument that removing scope eliminates customer functionality and therefore reduces the perceived quality to the customer. I disagree. A misssing feature, when expected, is not a lack of quality, but a reduction in value. Even this is tenuous—if the value is not present previously, or available in competing products, it's neither a reduction in value (as it never existed) nor a change in quality, because there isn't a feature to measure. What we do see in the wild is reducing scope followed by a low-quality release. Why? Well, it's not the scope reduction (doing less work), it's what we can't see—which is a stressed-out product development team, overwhelmed at even the reduced scope requirement analysis, development, and testing. It started with a competent idea to use lossless project compression (with scope) and ended up executing lossy compression by eliminating quality from the product.

Another way to compress a project schedule is bringing better talent to the project. Not everyone is equal, and a product manager with ten years of experience is often much more productive than one with two years of experience. The same goes for the development team, where an upgrade in individual talent proliferates learning and execution across teams. Parallel work streams may also be considered to eliminate low-hanging fruit at a rapid pace so that the more complex, harder problems can be given the attention they deserve. I'm not sold on this theory, but it's popular. I believe prioritizing the hardest work first leads to the best outcomes, but again, it will depend on the overall project design, which is not one-size-fits-all.

The last worthwhile solution is accelerating the connectivity of the software development process by using doubles. The terminology for this idea is broad; sometimes it's fakes, mocks, simulators, proxies, harnesses, etc., all with the same meaning: substitute a yet-to-be-fully-built software component with one that looks like it's working but just returns prescribed data. There is a saying in software that if it looks like a duck and quacks like it's a duck, then it's a duck. This technique is trivial to pull off and leads to improved quality outcomes, which we'll talk about more in chapter 8.

> "Quality is everyone's responsibility." - **W. Edwards Deming**

Strategies and Techniques to Increase Quality Through Project Design

Float

Remember Carl and the widget-to-sprockets integration earlier? Let's explore that more. Carl looks at the work required to connect the widget he built in Rust (the programming language) to the sprocket service (a web-based API). It's not that complex, but it's linear, with each step taking about one day.

1. Generate a Rust proxy for the sprocket service
2. Build test harness
3. Wire up connectivity
4. Write code to retrieve API results from sprocket service
5. Integrate results to caller service

In this case, the sequence is one through five, where each step has zero float because the next task cannot start until the previous task is complete. That's it. There isn't an option to do task three in parallel or step two and then one. Negative. It's a linear sequence where each step depends on the last step being completed—this is a dependency chain, and nothing is wrong with that. (It's like walking—left foot, right foot, all the way to the car.)

Float allows teams to create some flexibility in their schedules and accommodate for changes in requirements or circumstance changes. A requirement change is inevitable, so that's sometimes slightly baked into an estimate, but things like network changes may reduce the yield of a given set of tasks. For instance, a security scan shows that the last deployment of code to the development environment had a JavaScript exploit—this stops development until it's fixed because of how critical it is. A team estimating a lot of new, client-side code may build some float into their estimates to accommodate for the known-unknowns coming their way. The float here helps manage risk in addition to allowing the team managers to move hard to find development skillsets from one feature-based team to another. Finally, this float can be used strategically with other analysis techniques to reduce human stress and create conditions for the team where there is only one high-priority path at a time.

Critical Path Analysis

An easy-to-use but slightly time-consuming tool to reduce the impact of the estimation paradox is critical path analysis. Yes, critical path analysis is more formal project management, but it's wildly effective if estimating is taken seriously. And as we've already introduced, quality and estimation are linked, whether we like it or not.

Using critical path analysis requires a few things:

1. Required tasks
2. A sequence of the tasks, including dependencies and items running in parallel
3. Identification of the tasks that are either critical or non-critical.
    1. Critical tasks have zero float and must be completed on time for the dependent task to proceed.
    2. Non-critical tasks have greater than zero float.

4. Time and effort estimates for tasks.

With these items in place, next identify the longest path of critical tasks (with zero float) that depend on each other. It will look like a thread through the project timeline, where these critical tasks must be done in succession, while other tasks may be done independently and some streams done in parallel. Project management books may spend dozens, if not hundreds, of pages on critical path analysis, so please regard this as a start point to reduce risk.

Staffing

Let's return to my discussion of this kitchen remodel my wife and I want to do. While interviewing the contractors, we noticed another interesting observation, above and outside them all having different estimates. It turns out, to no one's surprise, not one contractor wanted to bring all the tradespeople to the project on the first day. You may be thinking, "Well, yeah, of course that makes sense." But why do you think that when we tend to bring everyone and the kitchen sink to the start of software projects: No one wants to be left out!

It would be insane, and pointless, to bring a plumber, a floor installer, a cabinet maker, a cabinet installer, an electrician, and a demo crew for day one of work. Is day one construction or demo? Is it for electricians or plumbers? Can they run in sequence with demolition? There are many more questions to ask, and they all yield a similar answer—maybe, yes, no, and it depends. There is a series of answers for a series of questions regarding day one because if it's forced to be everything, then it's nothing. Let's look at an example of this in a software project below.

Being everything is the same as being nothing.

In September of 2023, the Neato Pita restaurant chain started a new project to migrate their current point-of-sale (POS) system to a new-and-improved, custom-built software app running on new hardware they planned shipping to restaurants in February of 2025. Rebecca, the program manager, along with Darnel, the engineering manager, and Chris, the product manager, met to discuss starting the work in October. This project team reviewed the scope and began making some high-level estimates of effort and time. They assembled a landing team, putting one architect and one senior engineer on the project starting October 2, 2023, to work through some prototypes and finish the requirements process with Chris. They were all unconcerned about the approaching date until Rebecca received an email from the UX and design manager, Shawn. Shawn heard about the project and wanted Raul to attend all the daily meetings and be part of the landing team. Then Shawn talked to Maureen, who runs the customer support team for restaurant daily operations—she wants one of her supervisors, Amrita, to also be part of all meetings and join the landing team. The same thing happens with Ben, the IT director, and Suzanne, the QA manager.

Now the landing team is six, from the original idea of a two-person team. And instead of moving fast, they are moving slow. Really slow. There are four more people attached to the project who are not assisting with the project sequence—instead, they are bringing in concerns and raising objections over topics that shouldn't even be reviewed until January of the following year. Now, the planned work for October is drawn into late November, the holidays in the US hit, and nothing moves until the new year. See figure 6.3 below.

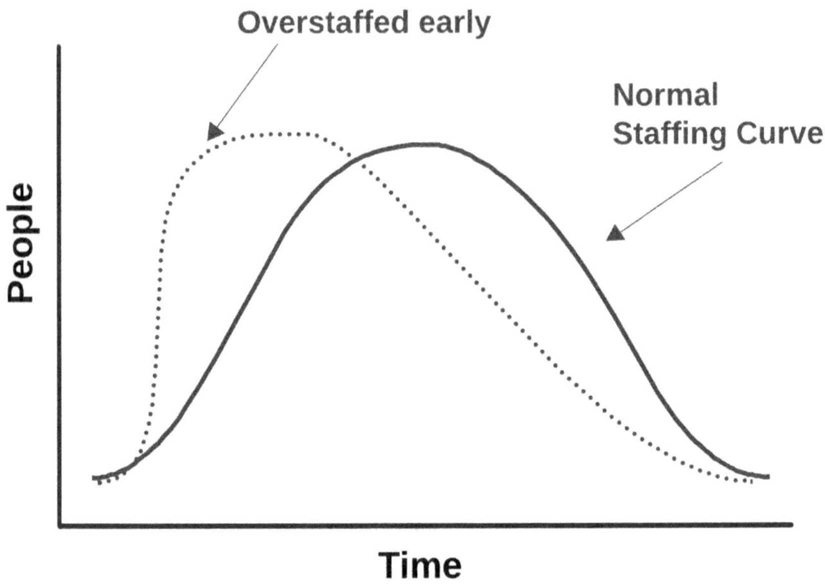

Figure 6.3 – Starting project with too many people

If you really want to kill quality, load a project with twenty people on day one! That will create so much confusion that no one will triangulate on quality. Plus, the costs will overrun rapidly, the project will go broke, and you can then turn a twelve-month project into a two-month project when the project is exhausted of funds and you're let go. There are a number of ways project quality can implode around staffing—but here are a couple favorites.

First, Death by People is when you start the project with everyone who will be in the lifetime of the project all at once, as what we just described above. Second, Death by Overload is when you ramp up the work on a project without adding additional staffing or the right skillsets, and the current staff falls over trying to balance the load normally accommodated for staff + N. To be fair, Death by Overload is reported by many software projects, regardless of staffing intentions.

In summation of quality and staffing are intrinsically linked when building (enterprise) software systems. Since software construction is a team game, not having the right players, like Billy Beane taught us, is not only correlated: It's causal.

"When you see someone coming to help you, run for the hills." - **Henry David Thoreau**

Incorporate Conway's Law

It is essential to recognize that the structure of your team significantly impacts the ultimate quality of your product. The design of the team should be considered a foundational element, rather than focusing solely on individual contributions. While it may not seem scientific, accurate, or fair, this principle holds true. The interactions within teams shape the work performed and the resulting outcomes. Additionally, teams that interact frequently are likely to develop closely coupled components, whereas teams with less frequent communication tend to create more modular and loosely coupled components. The nature of your product will determine whether you require teams to work in close coordination or independently. For example, a team developing an ecommerce payment gateway does not need daily interaction with a shopping cart team. However, during development, the payment gateway team should maintain strong coordination with security tools and procedures to ensure compliance requirements are met and to mitigate potential threats from malicious actors.

Both of these situations can be understood through Conway's Law, named after computer scientist Melvin Conway, who formulated the principle in 1967:

"Any organization that designs a system will produce a design whose structure replicates the organization's communication structure."

Therefore, accept that team design affects the outcomes and plan accordingly. If you need the components (or subsystems) of your solution to be loosely coupled, then stand up different squads such that they do not heavily depend on one another. Design your teams around the desired long-term system design and architecture, not the other way around. Designing your architecture around the team structure, or worse, the people individually, is a direct way to drive quality into the ground. You will end up with solutions that are non-conforming, testing will become arduous, and the code will bifurcate into unknown shapes and pieces as there is nothing holding it all together.

Set some domain boundaries, and these will drive the team structure. But what is a domain boundary? A domain boundary refers to logical system partitioning on business concepts or software modeled domains handling distinct responsibilities. Figure 6.4 is a simple banking example.

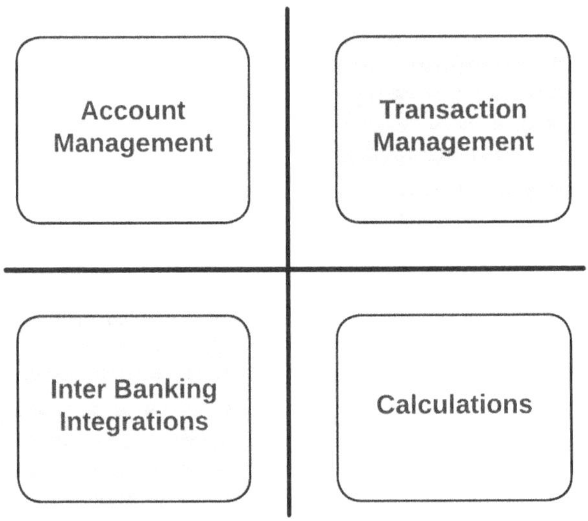

Figure 6.4 – Domains of a bigger problem

Banking Domains

The four core domains are essential to the system's architecture. Form teams around these domains to balance coupling, decoupling, autonomy, and interdependence. Defining these domains helps manage cognitive load. No developer or team can master an entire system, but dividing it into domains lets individuals focus on specific areas. This approach enhances quality and enables effective collaboration and integration. The aim is to facilitate parallel work streams, a concept that is often overlooked.

Parallel workstreams require a supporting team structure.

Now we are moving in the right direction—build teams around our architecture to naturally produce software which reflects our architectural demands. There are a few types of teams to accomplish working in these domains and crosscutting.

First is the value stream team, which focuses on the majority of activities and features outlined in the product management roadmap. This encompasses everyday feature development for a product—the essential work requested by customers or devised by the team to maintain competitiveness.

Next are platform teams. The term "platform" can be somewhat ambiguous, often referring to shared services, shared components, or core development teams. These teams build services and/or components that other teams require to perform their tasks or provide a comprehensive enterprise or SaaS solution. For example, a team developing an eCommerce gateway service, as previously mentioned, could be considered a platform team. Similarly, a team creating reusable Kubernetes and deployment scripts would also fit this category.

Lastly, there is the complex subsystem team, which is typically the most advanced and specialized among the team types. This team is responsible for the design, development, and subject matter expertise related to intricate areas that are not practical to distribute across various teams. For instance, core calculation services for financial services necessitate specific knowledge that is uncommon within a general product development team. This structure allows for the concentration of expertise, leading to increased efficiency and the encapsulation of complexity within a single area. Other examples of complex subsystems include image recognition systems in self-driving cars or the training of large language models.

Accountability Levels

Accountability is crucial for achieving results, and maintaining appropriate levels of accountability is essential for improving quality. Numerous maturity-level frameworks exist across various fields such as engineering, business, strategy, and human resources. Examples include the Capability Maturity Model, Agile ISO, and Business Process Maturity Model. Each field has its own set of preferred maturity steps developed by experts.

The software industry saw a proliferation of these frameworks until around the mid-2000s due to the dominance of Agile methodologies, which was discussed in detail in chapter 5. At this juncture, the pertinent question is how to accurately assess the operational maturity of a team, multiple teams, or an entire organization in a meaningful way. One effective method is to observe and document levels of accountability. The table below outlines these levels with examples from two distinct teams.

The first team, Team Zoo, is tactical with a myopic focus on creating and developing against set requirements where those requirements attain a goal for the customer. (See figure 6.5 below.) They are not focused on a platform or general problem solving. They certainly are not interested or mandated to acknowledge customer innovation.

<table>
<tr><td>1</td><td>Construct exactly to requirement(s).</td><td rowspan="2">Team Zoo</td><td rowspan="3">Team Lander</td></tr>
<tr><td>2</td><td>Build something that attains a goal.</td></tr>
<tr><td>3</td><td>Generate immediate revenue.</td><td></td></tr>
<tr><td>4</td><td>Solve a problem for a customer.</td><td></td><td></td></tr>
<tr><td>5</td><td>Discover new ways or working for customers.</td><td></td><td></td></tr>
<tr><td>6</td><td>Build software towards a greater platform outcome.</td><td></td><td></td></tr>
</table>

Figure 6.5 – Team Topologies

Team Lander, the second team in the table, has additional accountabilities to generate immediate revenue. The difference is subtle, but important: Lander will make changes to scope, requirements, and timelines to hit those revenue goals, while Team Zoo has discrete, specific work without the additional pressures of apparent financial rewards.

For instance, Zoo develops software supporting a new financial regulation that goes into effect eight months from the start of planning. They are responsible to take action, answering the status of the work and being the dependable part of the puzzle to deliver functionality into the market. Customers know the timeline, the scope is visible, and the requirements are set—the features developed meet the requirements, hence the regulation, or do not. Completing the development work in three months will not let the sales team capture more revenue overall or revenue earlier. So, the team patiently and diligently works through the requirements, tests, keeps quality paramount, and achieves their goals over a specified period—at less stress and low cognitive load.

Neither team is concerned about iterative learning, discovering new ways to work, or a larger more comprehensive platform—not because it's not important, but because it's not what they are accountable for. When every team thinks they are there to change the world, transform the company, or be a change agent, nothing gets done. Political fighting happens over turf and power, but there is just as much squabbling over what is right in subjective terms outside of the tactical, revenue, and profit realities that drive business. After all, there is a reason that senior executives don't get involved in the day-to-day operations and development of their revenue products...because it's people, and people are messy.

Quality is free, but only when addressed, directly or indirectly. I've seen too many times where leaders and their teams swap "learning," being "agile," and internal equity in place of a quality product customers want to use.

In figure 6.6 below you'll see the same rows with Team Astro occupying three different rows of accountability—solving customer problems, discovering new ways of working, and building platform-focused software. Astro operates differently than Zoo or Lander, but this says nothing of any team's importance to the company; they are just doing different work. Astro isn't focused on new financial regulations; they are integrated with a consultancy team looking at how they can evolve their product and take market share from competitors. So of course they aren't delivering strict feature-complete and tested features to production—they are accountable for the future. For now. These ideation sessions are often short-lived, reaping some return or notching up the expense column for the year.

1	Construct exactly to requirement(s).	
2	Build something that attains a goal.	
3	Generate immediate revenue.	
4	Solve a problem for a customer.	
5	Discover new ways or working for customers.	Team Astro
6	Build software towards a greater platform outcome.	

Figure 6.6 – Team Topologies Again

The vertical layers across accountability swim lanes are more fluid than a static illustration. Product development occurs continuously and at various levels. The work is nested and fractal, making it common for a platform team to contribute to the delivery of revenue-generating features or other practical situations.

Summary

Project design is as important to overall project success as the skills, talent, people, and technology deployed against a project objective. Project design is not expensive, because it's a choice among many options. The more appropriate the project design, the higher the quality of the solution. The key elements of the process are planning, estimating, critical path analysis (dependency management), judicious use of task float, staffing considerations, and time-cost management.

Takeaway

Billy Bean didn't win the World Series that year. They didn't even make it to the World Series—but they didn't have to, because the success found in transforming that team from a diamond in the rough to a polished diamond was enough. The same goes for the projects we take on—they can't be perfect, because they don't need to be perfect. It's impossible to achieve perfect project design, staffing, design, defect management, team morale, a flawless security posture, and dependencies lined up like the belt of Orion in the northern sky. It's just like defects—a thousand mean trouble, but zero doesn't mean anything. We want our projects to succeed, which does not require winning a championship.

Capturing quality without extra spending takes project design. Designing the project takes restraint. The next chapter makes a case for getting things done while keeping quality high.

7 - Control Patterns & Failing to Steer

Volkswagen, the German automaker, on September 3, 2015, confessed to the US Environmental Protection Agency that they purposefully installed "defeat-device" software in vehicles to produce emission-test-passing results. This ruse was in the making for almost a decade.

In 2006, Volkswagen aimed to boost its US market share and become the world's largest carmaker by leveraging fuel-efficient diesel engines to compete with Toyota. However, its new diesel motor failed to meet stringent US emissions standards. At a November 2006 meeting in Wolfsburg, Germany, executives decided to install illegal "defeat device" software that activated pollution controls only during emissions tests, allowing cars to pass while emitting higher pollutants during normal driving to reduce engine wear. By late 2008, Volkswagen launched a "clean diesel" marketing campaign, promoting models like Golfs and Jettas as eco-friendly alternatives to hybrids. Despite introducing advanced emissions technology in Passat sedans by 2011, the company continued using the cheating software to minimize maintenance costs, misleading both customers and regulators.

The deception unraveled in 2013 when West Virginia University researchers, funded by a $70,000 grant, found that Volkswagen diesel cars emitted excessive nitrogen oxides during real-world driving. A 2014 memo warned executives, including then-CEO Martin Winterkorn, of potential regulatory scrutiny, but Volkswagen provided false data to the California Air Resources Board (CARB) and attempted a software recall in 2015 that failed to resolve the issue. Under mounting pressure, Volkswagen destroyed incriminating documents before confessing to the EPA and CARB on September 3, 2015. The scandal, publicly revealed on September 19, led to Winterkorn's resignation, a $14.7 billion US settlement in 2016, a $4.3 billion fine in 2017, and additional settlements totaling over $21 billion. German prosecutors investigated thirty-seven individuals, including

Winterkorn, while Volkswagen engineer and supplier Robert Bosch faced legal consequences, highlighting the severe financial and reputational fallout from prioritizing market goals over ethical compliance.

Product development requires control mechanisms and steering beyond project management and development methodology. Long-term success is based on quality, purpose, performance characteristics, and measurement management.

Establishment via Discovery Pattern

A common control pattern evolution is establishment via discovery. Here, teams working in a new domain area work together closely, but as they narrow down the scope and complexity into manageable, idea-sized chunks, they collaborate less. Eventually, the teams require almost no collaboration. It may not appear to be a quality control pattern, but it is—just without the feeling of control. Indeed, establishing a pattern where the appropriate actions and behaviors are somewhat presumed to occur allows them to do just that.

Consider a team building a new SaaS product. They require cloud, infrastructure, and security support, which correlates needs of product development together. They wanted a platform to build more SaaS products, but if they extract the platform too early, it will bring product development to a crawl and deliver a platform that won't meet any future needs because its initial development was narrowly sliced on a single product. This pattern pushes the decision-making down and promotes quality by causally eliminating poor decisions before they happen.

"Next to doing the right thing, the most important thing is to let people know you are doing the right thing." - **John D. Rockefeller, Sr.**

Overloaded

Cognitive load references the effort required by our brain to process information in working memory. It's very much like object-oriented software—some objects are on the heap and others are on the stack. There are three main components of this load:

- Intrinsic cognitive load refers to the complexity of information one is learning
- Extraneous cognitive load references the presentation of information and how it may distract learning; it's about the manner of presentation
- Germane cognitive load is the effort required to turn new information into stable, consistent, long-term memory

Cognitive load starts to affect design, quality, and testing as it's wearing your brain down, and it becomes the same problem for internal or external testing. Software quality management is harder than playing chess because we play with imperfect information, with a virtual board that is constantly resizing. This complexity is why a decision to ship low-quality software to save time always boomerangs. The low load tactics leads to the destruction of the development process, the quality process, and introduces more emergencies while bringing morale down.

There is a concept called the size/complexity dynamic which states ambiguous or ambitious requirements can overload even the best minds. You can see an illustration of that dynamic in figure 7.1 below.

In sum, holding models in our heads and committing even parts of them to long-term memory is exhausting.

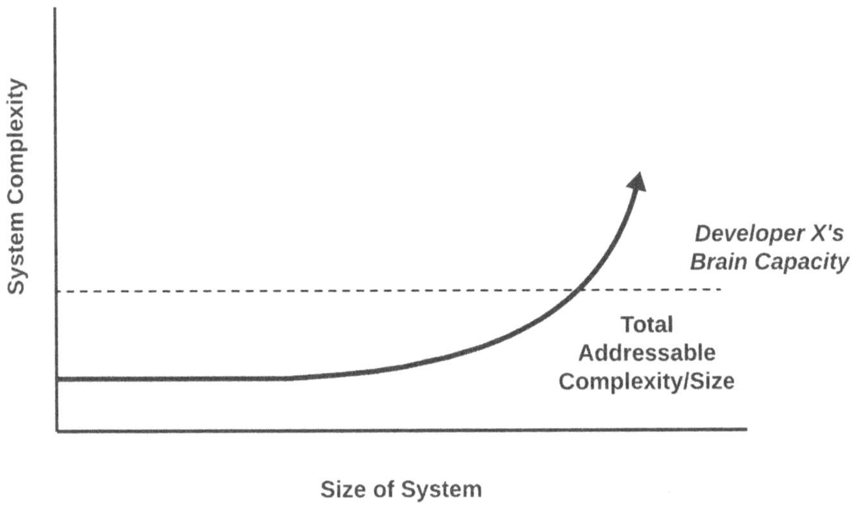

Figure 7.1 – Cognitive load

Evidence of Instability

As an industry, we are building systems and frameworks for software developers to use at a frenzied pace—more so now than at any other time since the invention of the personal computer. Every day, it seems, there is a new framework, product, project, or general murmuring around some advancement in software development. Look at NPM (Node Package Manager) and you will see more than one million packages. Then we have the ecosystems around Python, .NET, Java, and the growing Rust community.

All of these libraries equate to more plumbing, more plumbing, and more plumbing, enabling product teams to move fast because they are leveraging such a significant amount of prebuilt functionality. But the cost is coming.

Our world's security threats grow daily, and supply chain attacks grow. This fast iterative approach is starting to have real-world effects, and not just for complex industries, but for everyone, because the code that is in production today is shrouded in secrecy. What is worse, a vendor saying their libraries are confidential, or 327 build dependencies to construct a web app? The product now ships 327 components of unknown origin. And any of these dependencies can change at anytime—and the development team has no idea, and now the security team is trying to track down links in the supply chain.

Why do they have no idea? Because that's the intention of these large package managers and build systems—to abstract away and hide the complexity of building software. This is the supply chain of software, and it's one the most dangerous parts of the modern software product development process.

Let's look at how these problems come into play. Our industry has a hard time telling the truth. The truth is the majority of "product development" is some type of maintenance, or small feature development, on existing products. One doesn't need to discover and connect with users when the software offered is built into customers' internal workstreams. This type of development, though the majority of activity, has risk because the eyeballs and systems monitoring the code are less stringent than the big shiny new go-to-market product coming down the pipeline. Who are bad actors going to attack? The product under the spotlight, or the tech systems sitting in the shadows? Hackers aren't as distracted by shiny objects as product development teams.

These distinctions are important because customers need what they pay us for to work, all the time, securely, and not too slowly. Here, I didn't even say fast. Fast is for new products, with new expectations and market competition. Customers (businesses in the context of this writing) say they want fast and amazing, but when the board pushes back and *The Wall Street Journal* is covered in articles of foreign government and private group hacking attacks, they will opt for the solution that is secure, stable, and fast enough. Corporate boards aren't end users, and decisions for mission critical systems are hardly ever organic.

And it gets worse. The software industry will continue to suffer as security and reliability are traded for arbitrary development cycles and pressure to hit artificial deadlines. It's the same today as it was twenty years ago. Agile railed against fixed timelines. But the people who picked up the original Agile ethos weaponized the concepts into big business for themselves, replacing a two-year timeline with forty-eight two-week sprints—when the two are the same thing! Except now, we get a better ability to reprioritize, but frustration from stakeholders whenever features slip and slide because of non-functional requirements abounds like bed bugs in an old mattress.

Security and unreasonable development cycles are also why it's increasingly difficult to do business with smaller companies. Having certifications is helpful, but the trust will still be: does this company follow their SOC or ISO compliance certifications? It's fair to wonder if a four-year-old company, growing and turning over people, can maintain their HIPPA compliance when so many people are transitory or their primary concern is survival. Desperation leads to unintended consequences. These are the topics that matter. Who can get to market fast, and securely, when those two concepts are a dichotomy? Nailing these challenges down is what sells enterprise systems.

> We are a heavily constrained industry, by time and cost, and this will only become harder as the required security demands grows. There is only so much of the security monitoring toolchain which can be automated before that is attacked as well. Finally, consider this proposition: how can you move faster by implementing more "secure" libraries if you don't own the code in those libraries? It's turtles all the way down!

If it's good enough to put a man on the moon

NASA didn't attempt to design everything up front or measure velocity when trying to land on the moon. Nor did they wing it with experiments that would destroy equipment or lives. They found the balance needed and exceeded quality for their purposes. You now see that quality can come in many forms. And that over the years, quality is captured from the process without the tools we think are "the way" today.

Software Quality Attributes Through the Lens of a Dishwasher

Understanding Internal and External Qualities

Let us explore the essential qualities of software by comparing them to the familiar world of dishwashers—a staple in many homes, yet filled with design decisions that mirror those of good software. Each of these qualities, when addressed, do not require additional capital or funding—they are a way of working only.

Internal Qualities

Maintainability

The ability to efficiently identify and resolve software issues and facilitate ongoing development

Good maintainability means bugs can be found and fixed with ease, and future evolution is possible. For a dishwasher, this means easy access for repairs, widely available schematics, and replaceable components. Software maintainability is boosted by modular architecture and clear documentation, much as a serviceable dishwasher encourages longevity and reliability.

Readability

Clear and understandable for other programmers

Clarity and understandability by fellow programmers is vital for maintainable code. For a dishwasher, readability refers to the ease with which a technician or engineer can inspect and analyze its internal structure. When the machine is opened for servicing, a readable dishwasher will have its components—pumps, heaters, wiring—clearly separated and labeled, making troubleshooting and modifications straightforward.

Reusability

The ability to efficiently reuse code for comparable tasks, as well as the extent of modifications required for adaptation, collectively define its adaptability

Adaptability and the facility to repurpose code are hallmarks of good software. The dishwasher analogy translates this to the ability for manufacturers to reuse design elements or modules in multiple appliances. A standard water pump or timer could be integrated into other kitchen devices, demonstrating the value of modular design.

Succinctness

Minimizing code for a specific task

Writing code as briefly as possible for a given task can sometimes undermine clarity, leading to obscure and hard-to-maintain solutions. While succinct code may seem efficient, it often sacrifices readability and maintainability, much like a dishwasher built with unnecessarily compact or convoluted internal layouts would complicate repairs.

Testability

The capacity to develop tests efficiently, ensuring they can activate all pertinent program behaviors and accurately observe their outcomes

Software should be easy to test, allowing all relevant behaviors to be triggered and observed. To test a dishwasher, one might run cycles with temperature and water flow sensors installed, evaluating whether the machine properly adjusts for different load sizes or soil levels. Success is measured by how closely its performance matches the expected specifications.

The internal qualities are vital for efficient, high-quality, and cost-effective development cycles. I started with the internal qualities because they are often overlooked, traded off for the system and product experience. So now let's look at the external qualities.

External Qualities

Efficiency

Sufficient resource use

Resources must be consumed judiciously. Efficiency in dishwashers is measured by how quickly and economically they clean dishes—using minimal water and electricity. Software, on the other hand, must efficiently manage time and memory, and occasionally other resources like network bandwidth or storage. Design choices often involve trade-offs; a faster dishwasher may use more water, and a speedier program may require more memory.

Robustness

Ability to handle errors or unexpected conditions, including missing resources

A robust system handles incorrect inputs or unexpected external conditions gracefully. A robust dishwasher will not malfunction if loaded with oversized pots or if the wrong detergent is used. It features safeguards—like overflow protection and error alerts—to prevent failures under adverse conditions. In software, robustness is often bundled with reliability, ensuring sustained operation even when facing the unexpected.

Correctness

Adherence to defined objectives, also referred to as requirements or specifications

Software must deliver the agreed-upon functionalities as specified by the client or user. A correct dishwasher must reliably clean dishes as promised, regardless of personal opinions on what constitutes "clean." Likewise, software is correct when it meets the functional requirements set forth in its specifications.

Usability

A measure of how much effort is required to learn and use software in order to accomplish desired tasks: refers to the ease with which it can be used

Effortlessness in learning and using software, and achieving its goals, marks high usability. Dishwashers today are designed for intuitive operation: simple controls, clear cycle options, and easy loading. Similarly, software usability depends on thoughtful user interface design, often guided by human-computer interaction and user experience principles.

Other Insights

Every June, I visit the optometrist for an eye exam. Despite having 20/20 vision, I face challenges reading up close or working at a computer. Issues like macular degeneration, hyperopia, or color distortion can affect clarity, even when distant objects remain sharp for me. Just as software and dishwashers benefit from thoughtful design, so too does our approach to maintaining personal well-being.

Buffet of Metrics No One Wants to Eat

When we vacation as a family it's just a matter of time until we run into a buffet. And what an experience—would you like some salad? Yes. Spinach, iceberg, romaine, or mixed greens? Would you like some croutons, onion, chives, or cheese? How about protein—some diced ham or egg? And then a dressing—thousand island, ranch, peppercorn, garlic cream, oil, vinegar, or balsamic? Pizza, chicken, pot roast, dumplings, stir fry, rice, shrimp, meatballs, or lamb chops? It's amazing, absurd, overwhelming, and, often, truly useless. When my son was young, he would just get a chicken finger, mac-n-cheese, and cookies.

A software team can measure and use a variety of metrics from the buffet to ensure quality and efficiency of their testing processes. Here is a smorgasbord of items from that list:

1. **Escaped Bugs**: The number of bugs not detected during testing and found by users after release.
2. **Test Coverage**: The percentage of the codebase that is covered by automated tests.
3. **Defects per Requirement**: The number of defects found per requirement, helping to identify areas needing more attention.
4. **Test Effort**: The amount of time and resources spent on testing activities.
5. **Test Reliability**: The consistency of test results over multiple test runs.
6. **Time to Test**: The average time taken to execute tests.
7. **Test Cost**: The total cost associated with testing activities.
8. **Cost per Bug Fix**: The cost incurred to fix each bug.
9. **Defect Distribution Over Time**: Tracking the number of defects found over different periods.
10. **Test Case Effectiveness**: The percentage of test cases that successfully identify defects.
11. **Defect Leakage**: The number of defects that slip through testing and are found in production.
12. **Test Case Productivity**: The number of test cases executed per unit of time.

13. **Test Execution Status**: The status of test execution (e.g., in progress, passed, failed).
14. **Test Review Efficiency**: The efficiency of the test review process in identifying and addressing issues.
15. **Test Completion Status**: The percentage of test cases completed within a given timeframe.

These metrics can help product teams monitor and improve their processes, ensuring high-quality software development. But which do you use? Which will help to steer the project to completion? The sad answer, to quote a good friend of mine, is often, "It depends."

It depends on what matters most at any given phase of the project, product maturity, revenue generation, or myriad of other situations. What you should always do, though, is choose something to measure. I like escaped bugs and testing effort. Lots of the others take time to capture, while these two will get any team rolling.

The Core Four of Non-Functional System Design

Our industry loves to forget about the actual software problem and put all focus on the fun, operational, hosting-cloud stuff. But great infrastructure and lousy code is still a lousy product. And fancy infrastructure that lacks meaningful specificity is just as useless. To combat that, steer hosting implementations with the core four of non-functional system design.

1 - Scalability

Scalability ensures that your application can handle more load without compromising performance. Vertical, horizontal, or service-based.

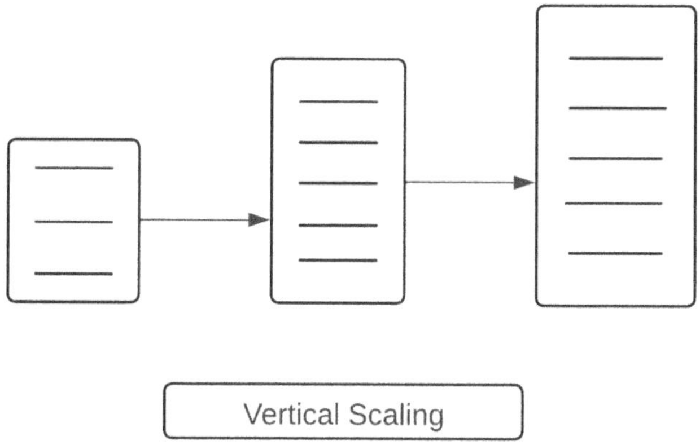

Figure 7.2 – Vertical Scaling

2 - Availability

Availability makes sure that your application is always ready to serve the users and downtime is minimal. Load balancing, replication, and failover.

3 - Reliability

Reliability is about building software that consistently delivers correct results. Monitoring, logging, error handling, and automated testing.

4 - Performance

Performance is the ability of a system to carry out its tasks at an expected rate under peak load using available resources. Caching, database indexing, and asynchronous processing.

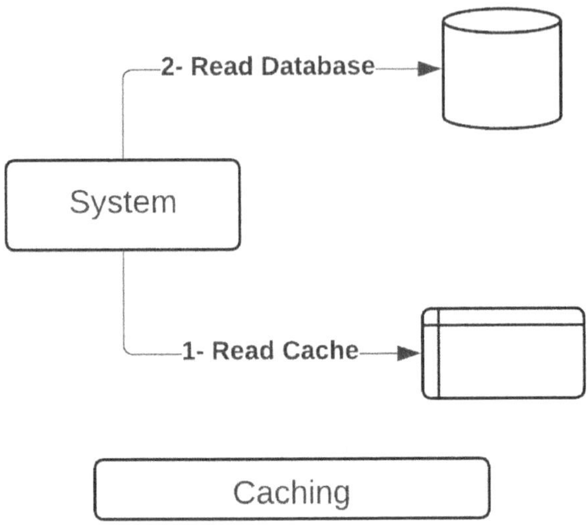

Figure 7.3 - Caching

Still

You can put these four together and still bake something gross. In cooking, one can take four expensive ingredients and make something awful. Anyone can burn a fifty-dollar ribeye steak. Amazing system design is just holding the line if the processes and decisions internally are incoherent or flawed.

Afterall, one bad O-ring blew up a shuttle.

An Example of Steering

Bill Gates, the co-founder of Microsoft Corporation, is known for his contributions to the technology industry. In the early 1990s, he recognized the need for a new operating system that could support more powerful hardware and provide better security. To achieve this, he hired Dave Cutler, a former engineer at Digital Equipment Corporation, to lead the development of a new operating system called Windows NT, where the NT simply meant new technology.

Cutler and his team worked tirelessly to create a new operating system that was more reliable, scalable, and secure than its predecessors. They used a microkernel architecture that separated the operating system into different components, making it easier to maintain and update. They also introduced a new file system called NTFS (New Technology File System) that provided better performance and security than the previous file systems.

Gates used Cutler and their teams to steer the largest software project ever taken on by Microsoft, or anyone else, to produce world-changing software. They focused on innovation through constraints, retaining the points of core four system design, quality characteristics, and measurement criteria.

Windows NT was released in 1993 and was an instant success in the marketplace. It was praised for its stability, security, and scalability, and it quickly became the operating system of choice for businesses and organizations around the world, overtaking their existing Windows product. It was also the foundation for many of Microsoft's future operating systems, including Windows 2000, Windows XP, and Windows Server.

Summary

We've outlined control mechanisms for product development, steering beyond project management, and development methodology. In here, we've examined internal and external characteristics that provide means for steering and control. And when applying controls to their metric measurements, we can increase quality without explicit quality focus.

Takeaway

If Volkswagen had used steering mechanisms and control patterns, they could have possibly alleviated their long-term challenges and manipulation. Long-term success is based on quality, purpose, performance characteristics, and measurement management.

Now that we've covered some control patterns and why it's hard to steer, let's jump into ways to make life simpler in the next chapter. Next, we're going to look at a way to systematize the software construction process end to end as we introduce the LIFT engineering system.

8 – Systematize the Start

The night sky used to astound and confuse people. Before Newton, the cosmos even puzzled the people who studied our sky—astronomers. Yes, planets moved, but their paths remained a mystery. Then, here came Isaac Newton and his seminal work, *Philosophiæ Naturalis Principia Mathematica* (Mathematical Principles of Natural Philosophy). In this significant book, he laid out his three laws of motion and formulated the law of universal gravitation. He found the connection by connecting the dots between the fall of an apple and the orbits of celestial bodies. Here, Newton revealed the same force governed both objects on earth and motions of the cosmos. Suddenly, the movement of planets became predictable, and science transcended the world around all of us. Newton didn't create the laws of motion—he discovered them.

Later, Einstein built upon Newton's discoveries with general relativity. Einstein didn't create anything either—he too discovered what was already present; in this case, how gravity works.

Science is full of discoveries that build on each other.

Discover this, then, two hundred years later; discover that the previous discovery was wrong. This happens over and over in science. For instance, in the fourth century BCE Aristotle supposed the earth was at the center of the universe. Everyone at that time who of course had access to this information and understood how smart Aristotle was believed his theory.

Next, in the 1500s Galileo provided an alternative to Aristotle. He thought comets were an optical illusion and that moons couldn't affect the earth's tides.

In 1687 Isacc Newton set the foundational laws of motion—discoveries that changed all aspects of how humans understand the world. Until he thought he could turn metal to gold and died of mercury poisoning through alchemical experiments during his time at the English mint.

All these discoveries were vital. But, we must admit, they were not all true. Aristotle's views were not correct.

Now, fast forward to today's enterprise software environments, where there are beliefs that practitioners alchemically attempt to transfigure into science. It's not.

We have stopped the act of discovery in the software industry, and this is driving up costs and reducing quality.

The world is stuck on a bunch of guys on a mountain in 2001 talking about manifestos to the draconian, documentation-heavy ways of producing software. And now, the agileists have become dogmatic intimidators. They have kidnapped helpful concepts and routinely shove them onto unsuspecting teams and organizations, using "coaching," which is another method for coercsion towards a singular viewpoint.

None of this is good for building high-quality software in a world surrounded by security exploits, growing data theft, and cyber terrorists entering the terrestrial world through our power plants, agriculture, and shipping. How will a Scrum solve the quality problems of today?

This isn't how science works. Science doesn't need someone to shout down at people about what works and what doesn't. And it's not how any other branch of industry works, with dogma running the industry.

Our natural philosophers, scientists, of the past discovered something worked—until it didn't. Aristotle was right—until he wasn't. Galileo was right about the earth's oceans being like a giant bucket of water sloshing around from the earth's rotation—until he wasn't. The approach to building quality, mission-critical software today is wrong.

Using a Software Construction System

This chapter describes a comprehensive process for software engineering called LIFT, which tries to back quality into the outputs. LIFT is not a process or a methodology. Nor is LIFT something you read and put on a shelf. It's also not made up as you go. This is a system designed to tie a series of activities together that don't often get the attention they need during the construction of software-intensive systems. A system is meant to be cohesive, helping you succeed at the business of constructing and operating software.

Not a Process

It's not a process for planning a product portfolio. It's not a process for identifying market gaps or identifying breakout ideas. It's not a process to accelerate user design or validate product ideas. It's none of these.

It's also not an open process that you then plug your processes into. It's not sAFE or scaled Agile, it's not Scrum or Lean or Kanban. It's not an Agile process or framework at all.

System

It's a system for building software that works. Constructing software. Testing it. Managing change. Releasing software. And then operating the software. That's it. LIFT is concerned with how the activities are accomplished so that they are repeatable.

LIFT is made up of the following evolutions.

1. Plan
2. Build
3. Test

4. Release
5. Operate
6. Manage

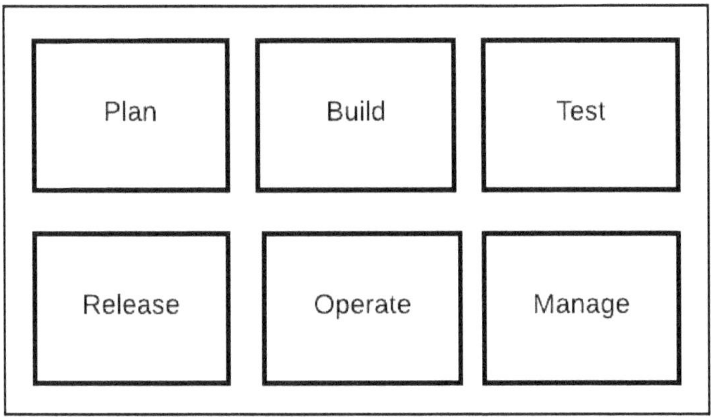

Figure 8.1 - LIFT Evolutions Overview

Each evolution is made up of a series of activities. *How these activities are performed, the details of each, and when to do them is the primary purpose of LIFT.* Executing any one of these evolutions on their own will give you benefit from where you are today. But it's how the activities are tied together into one system that will raise your team and provide material, long-term, repeatable results.

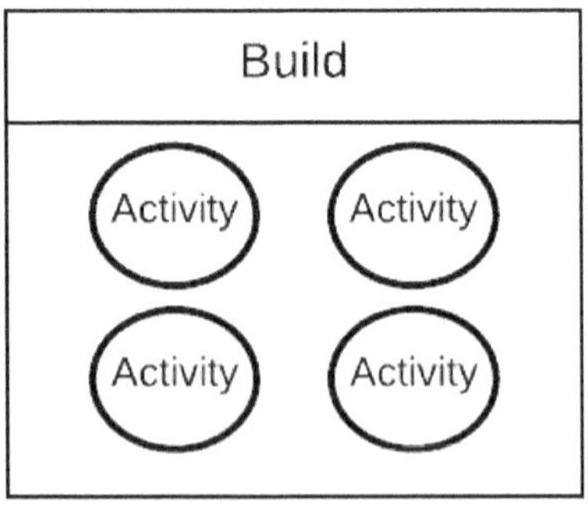

Figure 8.2 – Activities inside Evolutions

These activities are what LIFT is focused on because it is what is most variable between team to team and project to project.

Further, building software systems requires a formulated strategy. According to Michael Porter, a renowned American economist and professor at Harvard Business School, in his seminal work "What Is Strategy?" in the *Harvard Business Review*: "Strategy is creating fit among a company's activities. The success of a strategy depends on doing many things well—not just a few—and integrating among them. If there is no fit among activities, there is no distinctive strategy and little sustainability. Management reverts to the simpler task of overseeing independent functions and operational effectiveness determines an organization's relative performance."

Porter's examination of an entire corporation can be applied to a product engineering department, mid-size organization, or anyone building internal IT systems. Excellence at only the release portion of the life cycle, or the test portion, will not deliver big results. It probably won't even deliver the required business results. And if each link in the chain doesn't connect with the next, then the entire chain is brittle. Not having these activities clearly operationalized, systematized, and repeatable also means that the team will silo themselves. This then has managers attempting to optimize only their areas (development, operations, test), or exec teams trying to optimize for them and trying to then drive cost efficiencies. This will not lead to a competitive advantage. It just leads to leaner vertical, independent functions.

LIFT gives attention to all the pieces that make up the trivialization of software construction. Testing is difficult. Releasing is often complex. Operating a production system is hazardous. And managing the overall process and people to do this work is complex at the least and chaotic at the worst.

Thinking about software construction as six evolutions that make up one system cycle, which is then repeatable, gives this required formulated strategy a backbone to the entire endeavor of software construction.

Getting Started

Charter

Before we get to the evolutions of LIFT, let's analyze an additional concept which is very effective no matter the size of the project: a project charter document.

Don't let the idea of "yet another" document worry you—this one is written with the intent to reduce scope. Yes, this is the primary scope reduction document—and that is something to be excited about...so don't let the opportunity pass.

The Charter lays out the goals of the project, the desired outcomes, what isn't required, known dependencies, and risks. It provides a guiding direction for the team working on the project as the common understanding is derived from this simple document. Additional direction in this area is unnecessary because it's meant to be simple. You can download a copy from this books website.

Architecture

The topic of topics. Architecture. What is architecture, and what isn't architecture? Who makes these decisions, and how are they introduced into a system? LIFT is not concerned.

LIFT is concerned about two concepts of architecture, if and only if a change to architecture is required. This is:

1. The Current State Architecture
2. The Future State of Architecture

That's it. What happens with architectural choices, for many services, one service, no APIs, tons of APIs, monolith, or distributed system, matters very little. It's all execution details at one point or another. Wait, take a breath. It's okay—it really is just details when looked at from a high enough level.

The question is if the concepts can be captured into a view that will help the project team design, build, test, deliver, and operate the system, be it net-new or updates to the existing system.

Let's play this through just a bit. Let's say the new project, Project Boots, is a product with (1) one web front end, (2) one small API layer, and (3) one database, as in figure 8.3 below. The team analyzes the new requirements and sees that they will need to add a couple new APIs that are asynchronous, connecting to third-party services. Because of this new behavior, they will introduce these APIs into a different container from the existing APIs. Architecture has evolved, the core concepts are the same, but there are now new pieces, as illustrated in figure 8.4.

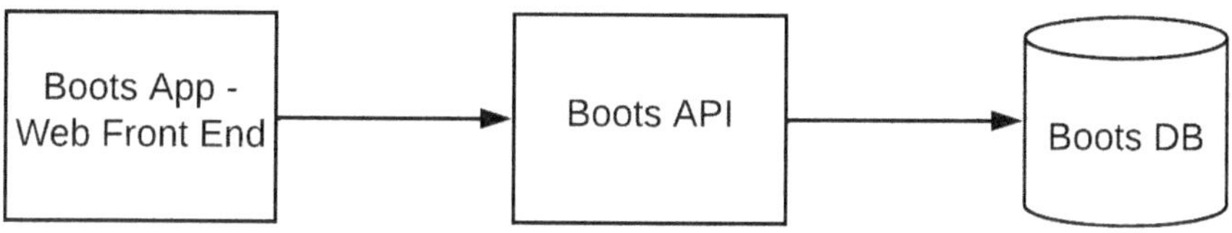

Figure 8.3. This is a super-simplified Current State Architecture view. Web front end, API, and a database.

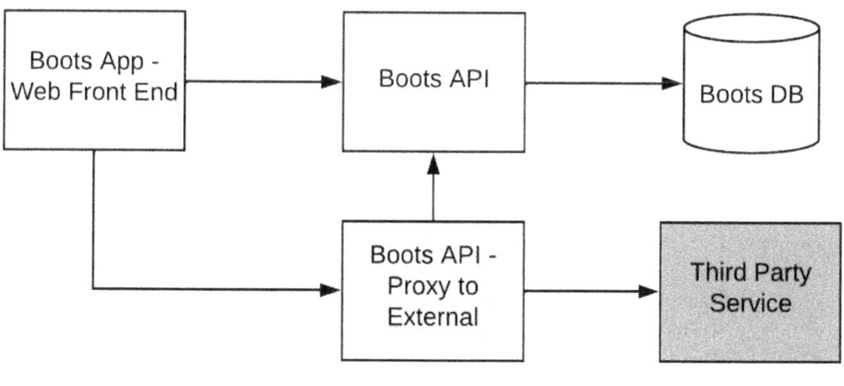

Figure 8.4. This is the Future State Architecture view.

Here, it's clear what the changes are because they are highlighted. Almost anyone from a junior developer to a group head can read something like this and grasp the change. From here, the discussion of infrastructure, security, and operations can start. This will win you many friends in your current team and your career. And, most importantly, it will set the project up for success by removing early project friction and confusion.

Like the Charter, another series of chapters could be written on Current versus Future State Architectures, so we won't go there. This concept is simple. Just let it stay simple and don't overcomplicate it.

Evolutions

Plan

The plan evolution in LIFT starts after the "we know what we want to build" phase of your overall product planning process. The planning here consists of taking a backlog of requirements, product desires with an architecture overview, and translating that into a releasable version of a software product.

The releases may be immediately consumed by users in a silent deployed state or released into an upstream integration environment with other teams. The point is, this is planning to start construction of one or more incremental software releases—not planning for a year or executing a portfolio of projects. The scope and focus are important for success. Success is in the details.

Target

Step one is to identify your target. What is your goal? Write it down and make it clear so everyone agrees.

For instance, "The target of this release is enabling our professional services team to configure the user management screens for a customer." This is challenging, has a purpose, and is not overly prescriptive.

Map it out

Step two is to take your user activities (or system activities, same in the context of LIFT) and map out a visualization of these. These activities may come from feature lists or a document of bulleted requirements for user activities. If you don't have this, then that's a problem, and it will be a struggle to proceed. These are part of the inputs to the plan evolution we are in. Go back and get them.

You can do the mapping on a whiteboard, stickies, in software—it doesn't matter. What's important is to capture the activities moving left to right on what you're trying to accomplish. Think wide and shallow first. This forms a backbone for the work.

Then, and only then, start thinking about and filling in the details. It will look a little like figure 8.5 below. There are probably cards that say things like:

- Wire up our logging library to login page
- Update deploy script for dev environment
- Show a static grid on the dashboard screen

Figure 8.5. Mapping out all activities that make up releases.

Now, the activities laid out above can be anything. What's important is capturing the activities so that light is cast onto not just the business functionality, but the work and activities to make these ideas come to life. This is an ideal format for engineers to express the need for non-functional requirements or simply capture the effort to get a minimum-ready-release state.

Finally, slice releases out of the work, where a release is working software delivered to your stage, UAT, or Live environment like in figure 8.6 below.

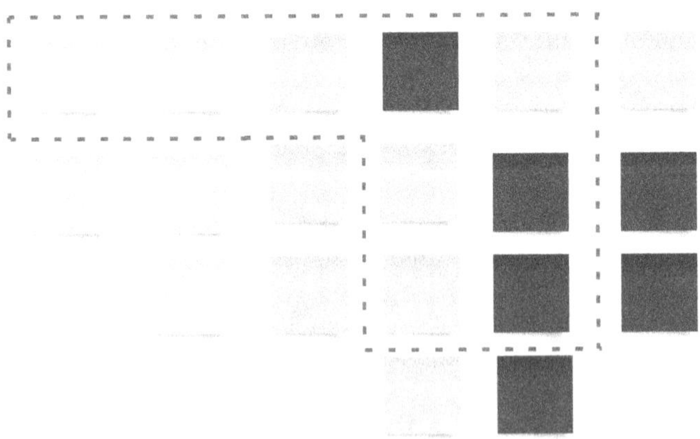

Figure 8-6. Slicing out releases from activity mapping.

Note: Why do we say Stage, UAT, or Live? Because every team has a different set of environments for different reasons, and those reasons don't matter. LIFT assists in filling the basics with patterns and proven steps. In this case, a team may have deliveries to stage and then, after accumulating two or three of those, feel like they have enough to go Live. Or maybe your product is already mature, and these features are going straight out to users. Either case will work.

There is an excellent book on this topic of planning called *User Story Mapping* by Jeff Patton. Notes on this book are in the appendix.

Now, if this is your very first construction phase of a new product, please consider identifying the absolute smallest product you could build which would exercise end-to-end functionality. Small. Like, really small. This is possibly a web page that says, "Hello world" with React, calling a Java API, that writes a message to a database that says "Hello" and logs the activity. Then deploy that to dev. Why? Because it tested *N* pieces of the system, proves your build pipelines work and that it will work somewhere besides a laptop.

Anti-Pattern - Flat Backlogs

When does this pattern show up?

Deep into a project's life cycle. Often in maintenance mode.

What is a flat backlog?

A flat backlog is a static, "flat" list of stories or tasks. It's a list of things to do, sometimes with some priority, but lacking any structure tying together how this work would be accomplished.

There is a fallacy across many non-developers that writing a "user story" will be sufficient to ship software. Of course, this is not sufficient. A user story never accounts for dependencies, testing, architecture, security, or new deployment requirements. And if the story does, then it's starting to break out of the scope of an easy-to-use user-story.

The agilists like to then say, "What's next in the backlog?" as if that is helpful to shipping fast, stable, and secure systems. This is the same as saying, "What's next on the list?" We are now trivializing the construction of some of the most complex matters of mankind to "Next on the list."

There are a few ways this flat backlog anti-pattern shows up.

1. The dev team doesn't know any better
2. An associate product manager is looking to keep themselves busy
3. There is a Scrum advocate at work evangelizing all work into backlogs

So, why would dev teams not know an alternative approach?

Backlogs are part of the classical Agile practices that've been co-opted by the Agile industry. So, many developers were brought up (i.e., taught and raised) to believe that this is how development is accomplished, and the only way. Consider a developer with thirty years of experience—they have experienced Rational Unified (RUP), Waterfall, Rapid Application Development (RAD), Spiral, all before getting anywhere near LEAN, Extreme Programming, or current-day Agile.

Next, we sometimes have junior product managers, product managers, bad technical managers, etc., whose only goal is flow. They fill up the backlogs nonstop because they believe it's their job to stay busy and keep "those developers" busy. Clearly, trying to stay busy is an anti-pattern for all business.

Finally in our list is the Scrum master. Scrum sneaks its way into teams and companies all the time because of the confusion between current-day vanilla Agile and Scrum. They aren't the same.

Big Rocks

Big Rocks is the LIFT way of interpreting the famous concept of "First Things First". Now, "First Things First" was not invented here. This concept was first written by Stephen R. Covey, a great thinker of the human condition and productivity (see appendix).

This principle is so basic, but so important, it's good to take a few moments to review using an analogy of filling a bucket.

- Big Rocks are the highest priority tasks and projects.
- Little Rocks are urgent items. You must do them at some point, or you'll get overrun by them.
- Sand is everything unimportant that doesn't materially move you, the team, or product forward.

So what does this have to do with developing software? Everything. The Big Rocks in your project are the most important and difficult tasks. An example of a Big Rock is "integrate the new Global Authentication System for Role Management." Or "build a proxy to the new Pricing API that returns under five milliseconds." This is non-trivial work! Most mid-size, three-to-six-month projects have at least two to three Big Rocks.

And the thing is, we must get after the Big Rocks first because they are the most challenging, will require the most effort, and have the highest risk of failure. Which brings us back to "First Things First." It's a waste of time to prioritize your schedule. You have to schedule your priorities. This is why the Big Rocks must go first. See figure below.

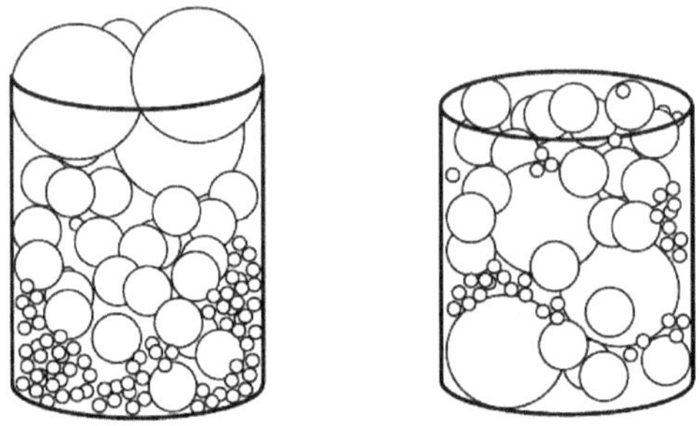

Figure 8.7. Big Rocks first

Like I said, it's simple. If the pebbles and sand go in first, the Big Rocks won't fit. If the rocks go in first, then the pebbles and sand can flow around it, and everything fits. Success with LIFT means putting the Big Rocks first and going after them intentionally.

"Effective leadership is putting first things first. Effective management is discipline; carrying it out." - **Stephen R. Covey**

Write the Stories

LIFT has adopted the Agile term "story" or "user story" because it's so prevalent in the industry. Substitute your own word or phrase if it makes it easier for you when communicating with your team.

Now that you have a few releases sliced out, write the stories. How you write the stories is outside of the scope for LIFT, but just make sure they are:

1. Actionable

2. Specific
3. Completable with the development strategy
4. Have dependencies called out
5. Are testable with test criteria
6. Entered and organized into your WMT as epics, features, or some other grouping. It's sometimes helpful just to put them all into a release.

Build the Sequence

LIFT Engineering uses all good tools at our disposal. A key, powerful tool is basic Gantt charts. A basic Gantt chart allows you to sequence work, show dependencies, communicate plans to stakeholders, and understand when things are going off the rails. You don't need to run the whole world from your Gantt chart (or call it a technical sequencing diagram if it makes you feel better…), but it will be invaluable if you are:

1. Building software with multiple dependencies
2. Building software with more than one team or functional parts of an organization
3. Building software with distributed teams
4. Building software that is time constrained

So it's almost always helpful. Here is an incredibly basic example in figure 8.8.

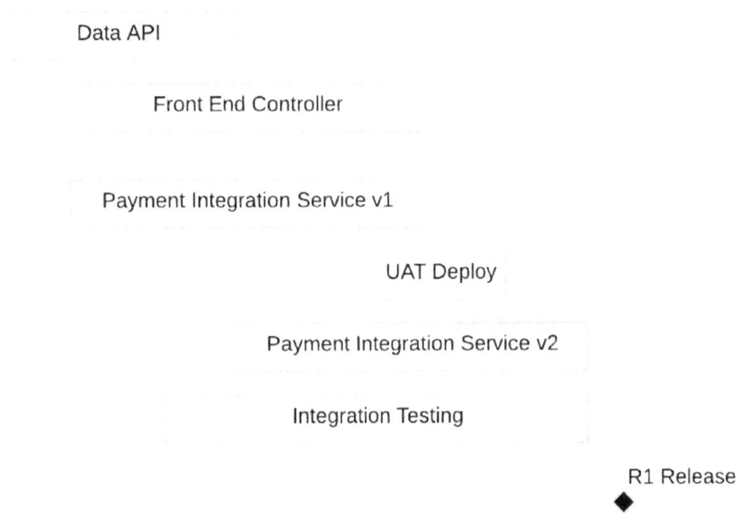

Figure 8.8. Gannt charts help visualize the sequence of activities.

BUILD

In the build evolution, the team constructs software using the best techniques available to them. LIFT is not prescriptive of how to write code. Here we will examine what most software looks like and extract patterns to consistently win this evolution. And even though Agile is not a panacea, some of the techniques are helpful and the terms are common enough not to redefine them—starting with what a sprint looks like in the LIFT world.

Anatomy of a Sprint

Few things cause more pointless disruption to teams than the fallacy of the two-week sprint. Even writing this is dangerous. There are legions of Agile practitioners and Agile desk jockeys who are arbitrarily tied to a two-week delivery cycle. Well, two doesn't mean anything. Why not one, or six? Look at earlier books on Agile and you'll see that—as learning to be Agile in mindset, practice, and delivery has nothing to do with compressing development and testing into two weeks. Let it go.

Therefore, to make the point, LIFT recommends three weeks or more.

Why three weeks? Three weeks allow organizations that have multiple departments and legacy overhead (again, LIFT is for all teams and companies, not fantasy teams) to coordinate. If your team could really use some extra time for regressions testing, some time to plan the next sprint and some remediation time, then more than two weeks is needed. I've seen consistent sprint processes of four weeks, six weeks, and two months.

The objective is consistent sprint success, and the means to this is consistency and discipline. As of this writing, I've seen the three-week sprint successfully increase quality delivery on at least five occasions, with different teams, different firms, and different cultures.

Week 1

The first week is about making active, meaningful headway on the most important development stories loaded up with planning. Planning for Week 1 happens during Week 3, so don't worry if it doesn't make sense yet. The overall goal of Week 1 is to develop functional software and attack the hardest problems.

Week 2

When moving into Week 2, expect to really start closing stories, getting test signoff on important items, and starting to think about the release. The release prep meeting is more important than it may sound. It's doubtful it sounds advantageous at all—well, think again. This session surfaces the details that can completely derail a release. If there is one place where an engineering team gets slammed by its stakeholders, it is botched releases—don't be that team.

Week 3

The third week is really about Week 1. Yep, now we are planning to start again, fixing must-have defects for the release, and physically releasing the software. Some of the planning activities listed below can be combined as well. For instance, some teams do not do the tasking session because the maturity of the team only needs planning and estimating. Then, when the sprint starts, they naturally order and execute the most difficult work first. Make sure engineers are driving this decision and not project managers, product managers, or Scrum masters. Engineers build the software and therefore order the work.

Non-Functional Requirements Pay the Bills

As software professionals, we aren't paid to solve business problems. That's just nostalgia from mainframe days. Old stuff you'd read in *Peopleware* or books leading into the turn of the century talk about "solving the problems of the business." Right. That's quaint.

We are paid to handle the complexity, connect the components, enable UIs, secure data, integrate systems, and deliver functionality that in turn incrementally puts the product and business in a position to grow. What is built must work across devices and oceans. It must be super quick, and everything that uses a mouse or a tap to navigate is compared to Google Maps or an iPhone.

How do we know this profession isn't all business "problem solvers?" It's so obvious that you'll miss it if you don't look hard. Global outsourced software development. We don't outsource, offshore, or nearshore to solve business problems. We do it to produce working software.

Produce working software and then trust that the product solves the problems set out by the product, leadership, and marketing teams. Working software to product and sales teams really means software that runs all the time, quickly, and as expected, or better. Working software to engineering teams can be inspected, debugged, observed, changed, and operated.

Quality-First Non-Functional Areas to Completely Own

What does it mean to own these areas? It means professionally making sure that the areas receive attention and are included in the build and construction of software.

The key non-functional topics for the BUILD evolution of LIFT:

1. Defensive programming
2. Heavy logging
3. Debuggable software
4. Performance

Defensive Programming

Write code expecting it to fail. Amateurs write software for happy paths. Professionals write software expecting it to fail. Professionals limit hubris and know they aren't omniscient. Expect your code to fail, software to fail, dependencies to fail, systems to fail, and servers to fail. Don't have servers? No problem. Your serverless functions can also fail for many reasons—like network or permissions.

So how do you program defensively? There are two primary ways: exception handling and guard statements.

Exception handling, for simplicity's sake, in languages like Java and C# are try/catch statements.

Aggressive Logging

Log like your life depends on it. Seriously—take it seriously! Imagine the derisive laughter of the team taking over after your departure when they tell their product managers they fixed runtime issues in the software you built because they added logging statements and then read them! Use this as motivation not to be remembered as a hack.

Being lazy isn't professional. It's an embarrassment. Here are five reasons to log aggressively:

1. It's easy to log.
2. It lets operators and others observe the runtime of a system with little effort.
3. Developers can get details out of their code at a scale that's not possible in local development.
4. Having log statements allows DevOps/secops/it-ops to construct other systems to make sense of logs, like alerts and events.
5. Logging is the simplest way to pull data out of a system with very little investment.

Questioning the validity of logging versus some other grand idea is excellent in theory. But why push against a technique so well understood and adopted? There are plenty of other challenges during BUILD without sweating something like this.

Small Functions

Write your functions small, as in short, so you don't end up with spaghetti code. It's that simple. No fancy refactoring or software patterns are required to do this, so even the junior engineer can contribute on day one. Functions call functions. Methods call methods. Rinse and repeat.

Avoid Coupling Components

Loosely coupled software components is the second key in debuggable software. It's a term that's thrown around at times by know-it-alls, newbies, or management. Still, it's a valid design concern and one that can assist with debugging software, so it should be respected.

The concept is simple, but hard in execution for new software engineers. Don't let the internals of Component A know Component B's internals. This goes into all kinds of design thinking around abstraction, interfaces, and polymorphic behavior—but don't worry about that yet. Just stick with A doesn't know how B works. A only knows how to work with B—but not what B does internally. This is accomplished differently depending on the language in use. In Java, this is usually an interface or abstract class. It's also achievable via naming conventions and data hiding in just about any language.

Anti-Corruption Layers

If there is one practice that can easily, and I mean quickly, be picked up by even an average-experience development team, it's the concept of anti-corruption layers published by Eric Evans in his book *Domain Driven Design*. *Domain Driven Design* (DDD) approaches software projects by thinking, modeling, and building around the domain using abstractions that work. This is different than the traditional object-oriented programming approach to modeling the real world with software. As we all now know, an e-commerce shopping cart doesn't mimic the shopping cart in your local Walmart store well at all. Software is nuanced and complex; a shopping cart made of metal is as simple as it gets.

Would you like the benefits of micro-service and distributed architectures like resilience, independent versioning, and deployment velocity without rewriting your world to micro-services?

Well, you're in luck, because the anti-corruption layer acts as a facade or intermediary between System A and System B. It translates what comes out of System B (someone else) into your language and data structures in System A (you). This prevents System B from leaking into your system, and that is more amazing than it sounds.

From experience, all systems, data, and APIs that aren't under your direct control are foreign forces with unclear intentions. That's right. Managing dependencies is serious business as your product's health and long-term maintainability is on the line.

Think of it like this: If you integrate the Foo API and your app breaks or is slow, it's your fault. However, the Foo API team has no problems. They are the service provider, and you are the user. Sure, the service provider has different stressors (reliability, uptime, versioning, etc.), but your failure is not their failure. Your product's loss is your product's failure. Period. So protect yourself because in software, no one will come to save you.

Is an anti-corruption layer additional work? Yes, of course, it's extra work. But it pays for itself very quickly. Generally in life, if it's too good to be true, it probably is. Will that new exercise bike make you lose twenty pounds? Not right away. Can you buy a stock that will surely deliver 300 percent gains? Probably not. So, you'll have to put your inner pessimist on mute for a bit because creating an anti-corruption layer to protect your system from another team's system will return significant gains. And it will produce those gains almost overnight.

Consider System A (e.g., your system/product/app/service) is responsible for calculating car leases' historical prices. For this to work, A must call into APIs from System B, which return the last three years' costs at different fidelity levels for all vehicles manufactured and headquartered in Europe. They produce data structures ABC, which have GUID identifies. This is not unusual, nor is it a problem.

However, System A also has to integrate with System C, a daily FTP drop of five-year prices for all vehicles manufactured and headquartered in Japan.

This integration has yet another data structure, and because they are sane, they use an increasing numeric value as their identifier.

Performance is a key non-functional topic because performance needs management one way or another. It either needs to get addressed for scalable support in system design driven by requirements or it needs to be addressed by requirements so that additional scale and performance is not required. Ignoring performance expectations is not a professional option in a world where most software solutions are delivered over the internet.

The Story Is Deployable

There is a difference between releasing a story and deploying it. Releasing a story means that we have put it into a destination environment of our choice and confirm that someone can use it. It doesn't mean it was successful! That's because stories in professional environments have dependencies. There are three items to cover: The deployment process can deploy the story to a target environment.

First, the code has met the standards set forth by the team. This is knocked out in step 1 of the DoD.

Second, any database changes required for the code to work are deployed into the target environment and tested. Why? Because a missing stored procedure will fail the code.

Third and last, make configuration changes required for the story to function in the target environment. Think of this as anything stored in configuration files/databases/systems. For instance, if this story's function requires a Feature Flag set to "true" in the config file, make sure this configuration gets deployed.

Eliminate Waste

The concept of waste is highly subjective. The product manager may say that waste is any work that is built but not released. The operations engineer thinks it's waste to conduct long releases and manual configuration. And, finally, the software engineer thinks it's all the meetings. So what is waste?

Beliefs

Table 8.1. An assortment of beliefs.

	Product Manager	Operations Engineer	Software Engineer
Waste	Unreleased Software	Long Releases	Meetings

It's all waste when looked at from a given perspective. But turn the view, and you'll see just how subjective these concepts are.

The product manager needs those meetings because she doesn't know if the development team understands the requirements and sequencing. So this is how it's done in her world. The software engineer doesn't choose to avoid big releases, because operations hasn't worked with them to decompose the production infrastructure footprint. And the unreleased software is a fact of life for both operations and software engineering because the requirements for them change too often from product management.

Now, none of this is true. It's just a perspective. It's no different than Plato and his allegory of the cave.

If All Else Fails

When planning, if nothing else seems to work with collaboratively producing requirements, return to default. Business requirements which lead to product requirements which lead to project requirements. Then execute the project. See figure 8.9 below.

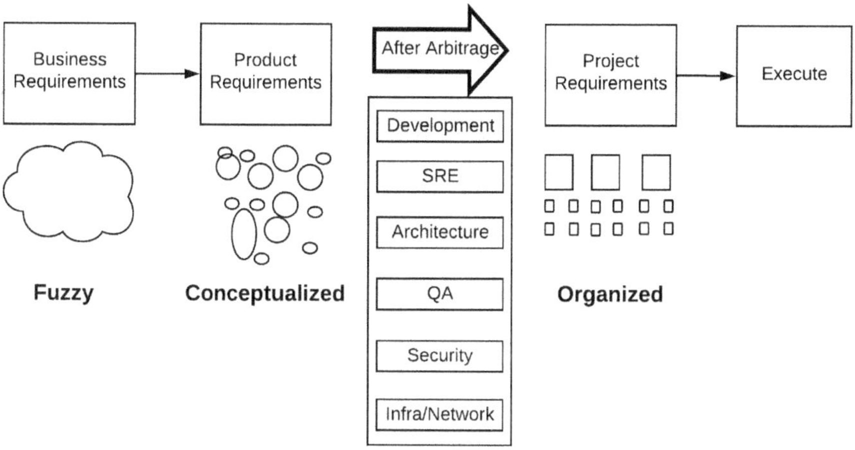

Figure 8.9 – Default Project Requirements

Summary

As we saw in the beginning of the chapter, if both Aristotle and Galileo were progressively, sequentially wrong about the earth and sun, then surely, we can accept that there are ways we've approached software construction which may not be correct. In the next chapter we'll focus on testing and operations.

9 – Systematize the End

What do you really want from QA and testing?

Most people reading this chapter in this book are not QA professionals. The QA professional lives on the fringe of today's modern business software development ecosystem. After all, the coding boot camps superceded by generative and agentic AI of our timeline don't include the outputs of QA engineers. Nor do our universities specialize in software testing, let alone what the industry calls quality assurance. Teams can enter testing phases casually and not be clear on their outcomes. Once you are clear on testing outcomes, then the steps fall into place, and friction is reduced.

Principles

Five key principles lay the foundation for the test evolution.

1. Document test cases and acceptance criteria
2. Maintain reasonable non-functional requirements
3. Keep the QA environment clean
4. Set and enforce exit criteria
5. Start testing before you start testing

Test Cases

Any given piece of functionality has more than one path for a user (or process, API, etc.) to take. Therefore, any user story needs multiple viewpoints, which make up the test cases.

Example: This requires test cases validating the currencies supported, null, zero, min-max, etc.

Acceptance Criteria

The current king of all test criteria is the vaulted, esteemed, much-beloved acceptance criteria. Acceptance criteria is part and parcel with the Agile concept of user stories. There is acceptance criteria for every story that goes into your work management tool (WMT) and with it, it is impossible to say if the story fits the needs intended.

Example: When a user enters a numeric value in the currency field, the value will automatically be reformatted to the currency set in their user preferences. The currency will be exact to two decimal places.

Set and Enforce Exit Criteria

Going back to the idea of "why am I testing anyway" comes this rough idea of exit criteria. See, it's easy to write some acceptance criteria for this example user story. Then map out some test cases, like null values, gibberish, form validation, etc. Exit criteria is taking all the work items that are rolled into QA and setting clear criteria on when the product is good enough to move out of QA.

Not such an easy answer, is it?

Here the team must get specific around defects, product owner decisions, and the non-functional requirements so that everyone knows what done means in QA.

Start Testing Before You Start Testing

This principle means that the build that enters QA can't be "thrown over the wall." The developers must do their best to test at the unit level (function, class, module, API) and have received some early feedback from the product owner and hopefully a QA team member. The code entering can't be littered with small issues as that will consume all the test cycles and everyone loses.

If the team doesn't start feature testing around acceptance criteria and non-functional requirements before you start QA testing, the likelihood of failure goes up dramatically.

The Testing System

The diagram in figure 9.1 below shows testing starting before entering a QA environment. This is the world's most straightforward development and test cycle. Code, commit, review the commit, deploy to a development environment, and run automated tests. For some teams, if they implemented only this cycle right now, their ROI from reading this far is complete.

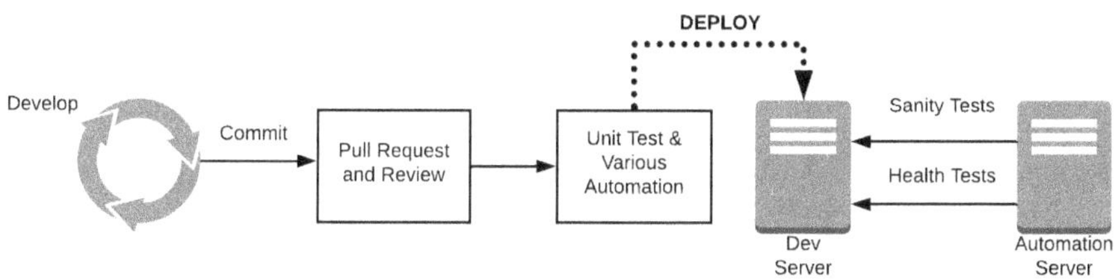

Figure 9.1. Testing that is being done in development and coming into QA.

The testing system is composed of processes and activities, just like PLAN and BUILD. As we know, every system has a beginning and end, so we want to start there. We're going to get into details on all of these, including the practices inside the activities. To begin, below is the high-level sequence of activities making up TEST in figure 9.2.

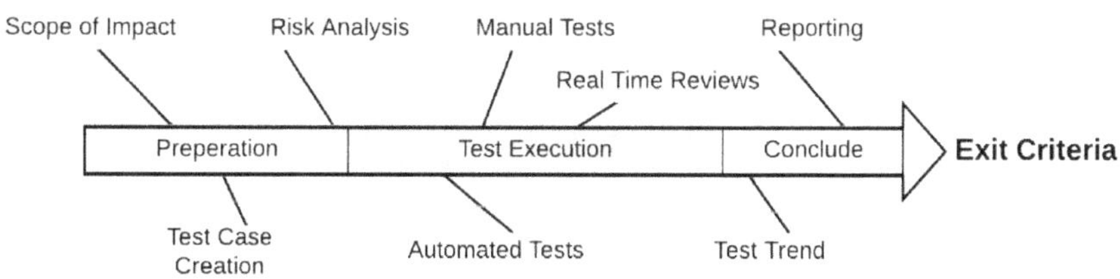

Figure 9.2. Steps inside of QA environment and exit criteria.

You'll look at this and maybe think "that's a lot of steps," and like everything in software, it is. It's challenging, detailed, and time-consuming work. Now it's clear though.

For software to get to production in a state that works well, you'll have to walk a journey. And even if you decide you don't want to spend this much time in TEST, these activities aren't going away. What you now have here is a clear sequencing of the activities for success. Let's get into them.

Exit Criteria

The last pre-requirement to enter the test system is a common, documented set of exit criteria. The exit criteria are the rules and covenants laid out, describing the events and successes required to move the build of software in QA to the next environment in the chain.

Exit criteria is very subjective to the product being built and the team doing the work. For instance, a team could have exit criteria like the table 9.1 below for a basic stock-trading application.

Table 9.1 - Criteria

Order	Criteria
1	All automated functional tests against the UI and Core trade types passed.
2	No new WARN or ERROR messages in the logs.
3	Every work item in the WMT and in the current build have their acceptance criteria accepted.

The exit criteria are not a release to production—it's just the team's requirements to move to the next environment, so it's lighter weight than what it takes to go live. Some product teams may have three items in their exit criteria and others may have a dozen—what matters is taking the time to define the criteria to protect the next environment, reduce false positives, keep the WMT clean, and increase the chances of success for going live.

Scope of Impact (SOI)

We look at the total impact of the changes to the system and from that point identity how wide the effects may reach. Think of it like an explosion with a blast radius like in figure 9.3. For a small explosion, the radius maybe ten feet. But for a large device the radius may be a hundred feet, and as we know, an explosive used in combat could be exponentially more.

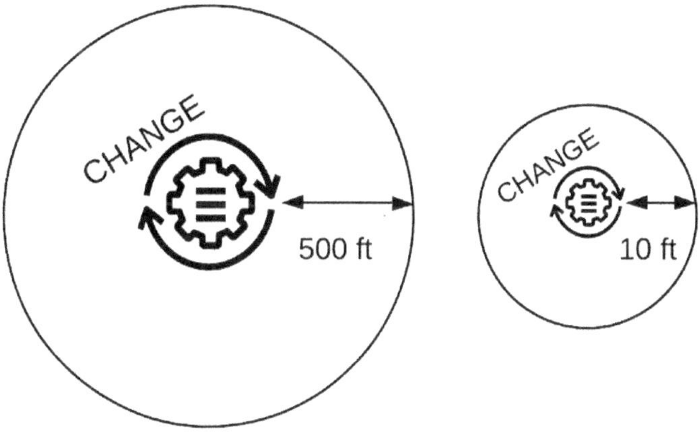

Figure 9.3. Scope of Impact

That is what changing code and configuration can do—ripple out and blast away dependencies and functionality without intention.

Wondering what this means? Let's look at an example.

The purple team needs to change the Pricing API for iteration 24. A couple dozen work items in the iteration are composed of small updates, some configuration from the security team, and two of the work items reflect adding a field to the API output. For context, the API has eight different end points.

Test Case Preparation

Test cases are not scary. They are highly repeatable documents mapped to acceptance criteria and existing known paths in the software. The QA world has its own language, and LIFT doesn't try to rewrite that language nor does it actively try to adopt it. Instead, LIFT is concerned with common sense approaches to testing so that teams have what they need to succeed.

Test Cases commonly come from one of these two places:

1. Someone writes test cases with the iteration based on the acceptance criteria from a work item. Why? Because the AC is the blueprint, and the test cases is the objective schematic plus an explanation of how the testers will perform testing.
2. A bunch (anywhere from ten to a thousand) of test cases exist and came with the team you have recently inherited or joined. Where this came from is a mystery that doesn't need solving.

As shown below, when the work item has AC, someone can write test cases off that AC. So if the work item doesn't have AC, then it's not testable. If it's not testable, why are we working on it? And if this is really the case, it's your job to make a stink about the situation until it's resolved. It is not professional to release software that is not testable. Just stop and figure it out with the team.

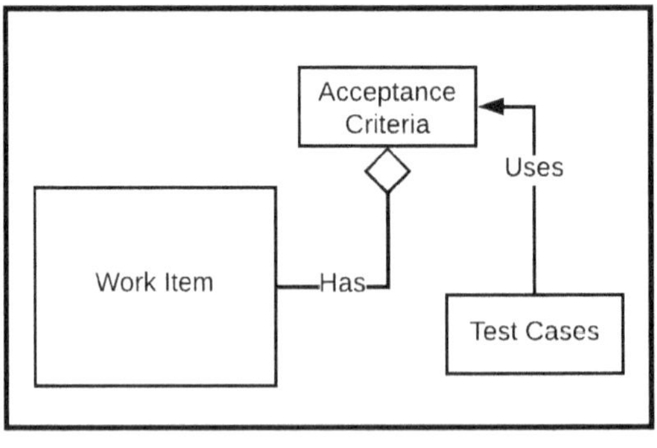

Figure 9.4. Work items and criteria.

Write test cases as documents, wiki pages, somewhere in your WMT, or best yet, in a test case management tool. All in all, getting the test cases detailed out in a wiki and linking it in the work item is a rather efficient scenario. But if you are moving toward the need for test suites (which is just a fancy way of discussing an ordered grouping of multiple test cases) you'll want a tool. Still, for LIFT, pick up whatever works (Google Docs, wiki, etc.) and use it until it doesn't work anymore.

Risk Analysis

Looking at the scope-of-impact and the test cases we have, what is the risk that these changes will:

- Not deliver on time
- Fail testing
- Cause production incidents
- Affect users or systems negatively
- Open other risks through dependencies
- Fail a security audit

The scope-of-impact on this work showed a large area of scope and possibly significant impact in several places that aren't changed or tested often. Without even writing more test cases (including the one earlier in this chapter) the QA team members note there are at least another couple dozen test cases for the website alone. Baking in a guesstimate for the other services, screens and internal tools affected and the number of test cases nears fifty.

Communicate the risk of a given work item or feature to the development team, other testers, and product managers using the matrix below. Every work item receives a risk level, and you should expect most to be "Standard" level. An iteration or release loading up with numerous explosive or flammable items is a clear indicator of danger.

Imagine a stack of boxes at your front door. Now imagine them again but on half the boxes put Hazmat stickers. Worried? You should be; that's why we measure risk.

Manual

Performing manual tests is okay. No matter what you've read or heard from peers, doing some manual testing is not an issue. Why? Because the world is messy!

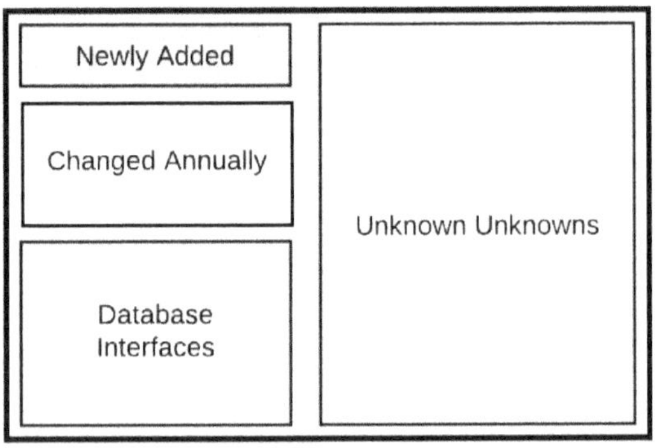

Figure 9.5. Net total code in the system

The diagram above is a ten-thousand-foot view of a ten-year-old home builder's item management system. This builder is required to keep track of all building materials used, their manufacturer, those items' source of origin, and the blueprints/plans they are associated with. The box in grey is some new code the team added to support building some modern home prefabricated inventory—basically, hold inventory from another supplier before it comes to job sites but will never enter physical inventory. The team added a new API interchange from this item management system to the new vendor to accomplish the functionality.

Then, another handful of user modules and code that everyone knows changes annually as some relationships change and material manifests improve. And next, there is a significant amount of database interfaces because, like so much business software, version one was a direct connection of user interface to database and grew from there. Finally, the box on the right is unknown unknowns, which is a fancy way of saying "everything else."

The team has two developers in Ohio, three developers in Mumbai, two QA testers also in Mumbai, and a subject matter expert from accounting in Ohio. No single individual on the team was present when the system was built, and the longest tenure is five years. The chance of inheriting a system with even 30 percent UI or API test coverage is close to zero. It's not bad or good, it's just the truth.

Therefore, the team is changing about 10 percent of the overall system annually and currently adding an overall 5 percent net new set of code for the new feature. They cannot reasonably write test automation over the entire system with the team size they have. However, they can write their new test cases with automation software and keep regression-testing the rest manually.

And this is the trick: Automate aggressively on the new features and cover the old, slow-changing features with manually executed test cases. Eventually, you'll make changes to the slow-changing pieces and can write the test coverage with automation. Or, frankly, probably not. Those slow features will not change, and when they do, it will be a blue-moon effort and possibly still not worth the time to automate.

Automation is happier with friends because automated tests build up into test suites, and groups of test suites yield power of known knowns. Keep moving to exponentially grow automated test coverage, and the manual testing won't really matter.

Release

Problem #1 - The act of releasing software is chaotic.

Have you ever had a team of exhausted engineers, testers, operators, and product managers at the end of a release? I have. And many, many teams across our industry have, so if you've not, you are either (1) in no need of help or (2) lying to yourself. Because in so many teams, releases are chaos.

Well, maybe the act of getting the software physically moved to production isn't always an issue, but everything after that is. The question is: What happens next? Just walk away. Have someone "login and validate"? Seriously, this is 2026, and that is so 2001.

I assert that releasing software for some teams is so stressful, so chaotic, and so full of dread that people burn out just from this last step. And this is a savage shame, because the act of releasing does not return value anywhere like the creation of new features does.

Problem #2 - You lack a system to predictably deliver solid releases to customers.

Your people aren't burned out from software releases? Well, excellent, you're winning. But it's still messy? It still takes more time than is intended and generates excessive noise in the teams and stakeholders. How about the notification that you send out saying "The Foo Bar System will be unavailable between 9 and 10 p.m. ET for maintenance"?

We all know there isn't any maintenance! You're releasing software, and it's unpredictable because you don't have a system. Again, it is not stressful out of the gate, but that's because the team is masking it by buying chunks of downtime every month. This too is not sustainable. Just wait until the FooBar System needs to be integrated with SalesForce, and it can't go down. Then what? A two-hour "maintenance" window?

And frankly, what the heck is software "maintenance"? Software doesn't need an oil change, or its tires rotated, so this is all just a friendly lie we tell ourselves.

Now that you know these problems, let's look at some of the possibilities on the other side.

Possibility #1 - Releases are non-events.

Think about it. So many software releases are full of stress and mishaps. But why? Software teams spend weeks, months, or sometimes years to build a new increment of software...and then the most important piece: deploying it to run for customers to generate revenue, and the whole stinking thing falls apart.

Really. It's a disgrace. Thousands of human hours of planning, managing, coding, testing, and configuring, and then the release is coordinated the day before and goes off like rollerblading down some stairs—just absurd and borderline dangerous.

Imagine if the release were just the last step. Another part of the development cycle that was planned thoughtfully, coordinated with vigor, and executed like a code check-in. That's how it could be.

Principles

Three key principles create the foundation for the release evolution:

1. Write it all down
2. Rely on automated tests
3. Not everyone can be in charge

Write It All Down

Like so many parts of LIFT, this too is straightforward—if you want to get it done, write it down. Consider the analogy with how people use paper-based planners and what happens with the anxiety and stress of a workday. We will use Sarah for our example, so with her, two things happen:

1. When she writes her day's plans down, anxiety (about the future) reduces, because it's clear what the plan is for tomorrow and the day after and, quite possibly, the day after. Are there changes? Yes, of course. But she knows what must go and what can stay.

2. Stress (about right now) reduces because it's clear to Sarah what she needs to do now.

How significant are these changes from writing her day down in her planner? Massive. Anxiety and stress are killers! And they run rampant inside of software development and operations teams, so reducing these in any way is an opportunity not to be missed.

But that's not all. See, Sarah will also pick up some of these key characteristics:

1. She's more motivated. Since her mind is clear from the noise, she has focus, and this focus is what individuals and businesses want from their team members.

2. She's more positive. If you reduce anxiety about an activity, make the activity easier, and increase motivation, then you would feel better too.

A software release is often like conducting an orchestra—releasing many different parts of a system from the database through the UI—and these take planning. Sarah writes her week down. The conductor has the sheet music and her orchestra positioned. It's all planned and written down.

ANTI-PATTTERN --- Not Everyone Can Be in Charge

When everyone is in charge, no one is in charge. And this means imminent failure for a release. Imagine this exchange on the night of a release:

Sarah: "Bill, go ahead and run the DB update scripts."

Kanna: "Sarah, go ahead and run the service deploy."

Project Manager: "What? Which comes first?"

This lack of coordination leads to exponential problems when the situation, like a release, is time-boxed. It comes down to "going off script."

Dependencies

Dependencies are everywhere.

These are all dependencies: database(s), another team's API, your APIs, a third-party component, or an upgraded UI library. In the build evolution earlier we looked at an example team finding they had over twenty dependencies while they thought they only had a small web application. The dependencies section of the ignition document allows you to list everything you consider a dependency that impacts the deployment or, just generally, affects the operation of your application.

Again, this is nothing fancy, it just gets the information communicated to facilitate other conversations or actions if required. Usually, for ignition, you can just call out dependencies that are changing. See table 9.2 below.

Table 9.2. Dependencies listed in the Ignition document.

Dependency	Owner	Notes
Calculation Service	Central Team	They released a new version last month.
Fund Database	You	We are deploying several new stored procedures and one index update.

Woe is to those who ignore their dependencies. - **Anonymous**

Risks and Mitigations

A risk is anything your product team considers dangerous or volatile that if left unattended has a high probability of derailing your deployment and overall release. A risk is exceedingly contextually specific.

Consider, your new version of software has a new JavaScript library update—a risk for this could be "browser compatibility issues in the wild."

Or maybe the release requires a dependency from another team to be in production before your release—a risk here is "cannot deploy onto the old version of the calculation service."

Risks are great to call out, and you'll feel a little relief getting the items that can generate failure recorded and various eyeballs on them. This is not the intention. In business, a risk without a mitigation is worthless.

What is mitigation? A mitigation is the act of reducing the severity or impact of a given risk. We are just scratching the edges of the broad topic of risk management. What's important to remember is that every listed risk must have a mitigation. If the risk doesn't have a plan to eliminate (to mitigate the risk), then the risks are just a wishy-washy list of complaints—and that helps no one.

Risk, mitigation, risk, mitigation—this is the pattern. Think about it: When Sarah the senior manager asks you if there are any risks to the release and you say, “Yes, lots...” what do you think she expects from you next? Do you think she will high-five you for creating a list of things that can go wrong? No! She will ask, “What are you going to do about them?” What is the plan? This is risk mitigation.

Release Checklist

The checklist is as powerful a risk mitigation tool as anything you will find. The checklist is used for everything from “don’t forget the milk” to-do’s all the way to “this rocket is ready to launch.” The inherent efficacy of writing down what needs to be completed, in order, and then checking them off a list is the way humans control variability and generate safe environments. In the release evolution we create a consistent checklist of what needs to be done, each time.

I worked in an industry called EHS (environment, health, and safety) for a short time in my career. We built SaaS software for companies operating with hazardous materials, large mechanicals, or warehouse operations. All these companies have people exposed to high-risk situations—being crushed, starting fires, or spilling hazardous materials.

For instance, consider an oil refinery. If you’ve ever seen one, they are maze of pipes, valves, and switches. To stop the flow of material from one section of pipe is not just pushing a button. There are multiple steps required, in a certain order, to be performed exactly, every time. The consequence of not following the checklist? Explosions, equipment damage, lost time, and bodily injury. Now, if you ran this operation, would you let the team do this type of work without a checklist?

In software, we bypass this all the time. We think Fred has a great devops mindset and skillset, and that his scripting and deployments will work the same every time and we can trust him.

Trust him? Trust no one. If you only take one thing away from this chapter, please let it be to trust only the process and checklist. People are liabilities.

Therefore, we automate testing. Therefore, we write unit tests. Don't get lazy on the last mile of a release.

Are you still not convinced?

NASA deals in nothing but complexity and safety critical systems. The below text is from the 1990 paper "Flight-Deck Checklists."

Checklists should contain, in abbreviated form, all the information required by the trained flight crew to operate the airplane in most normal and non-normal situations. Normal checklists should be organized by segments of flight. The checklist should contain the minimum twenty-two cues required for the trained crewmember to verify that the appropriate actions have been completed. Only procedural steps which, if omitted, have direct and adverse impact on normal operations are included. Items annunciated by crew alerting systems are not included.

Flight-Deck Checklists

The authors of this paper are sharing this from another association, the Air Transport Association, who has the same recommended philosophy as air-frame manufacturers (think Boeing) and all airlines (think United, Delta). They all agree—a flight crew needs a checklist.

We would not have commercial flights without checklists. Why? Because five percent of planes would have crashed annually during the golden years of air travel, and no one would fly.

And, finally, health care. In 2001, critical care specialist Dr. Peter Pronovost tried creating a checklist to approve one problem: line infections. He created a checklist of five steps that the practitioner will follow each time they change a line. They then monitored line infections in the department where the checklist was used and, in a year, they saw the ten-day infection rate went from 11 percent to zero. When they extrapolated those numbers out, it predicted they saved two deaths, dozens of infections, and over a million dollars in costs. All from a checklist.

Operational Quality

Operating a software system is often taken for granted as a secondary or third-level concern when designing and building new software systems. This myopic focus on build and ship, at the expense of quality and operating capabilities, is a key drive for what this book and system are all about. You'll see that operating a system in production is non-trivial but not complex. It too is a series of activities, concerns, and outcomes.

Problem #1 - You have no idea what your software is doing.

The software is shipped—yeah! Now what? How many errors are happening daily on connection to your internal dependencies? Is the software running as quickly and responding to the timeline as expected? Do you even know what is expected for response time?

Okay, this is easy stuff. How about the data? Are all your records being saved? Can you prove it? Most of the time teams have no idea if their production software is doing what is expected unless someone complains.

Problem #2 - There are no hooks to observe internal behavior.

A hook is a method that an external system can connect to and extract relevant information. You don't have anything like this programmatically, so it's not possible to, say, have your software call an external API on interesting events. Your software is static, not dynamic, so it is brittle to change and observation.

Problem #3 – Incidents and accidents just happen with little to no consequence.

The result of your inaction is telling everyone around you that you just don't care. You and the team are a walking generality with no concept of specifics.

The system is slow.

The page only partially loads.

Records are missing from the database.

A whole segment of customers cannot login.

All these things are incidents in corporate systems and SaaS, yet they just keep happening to your projects, and things only improve partially and slowly, and no one is ever held accountable.

Operating Procedures Drive Change

You see these principles build on each other and need one another. A software system is measured and then tested—in as many places as needed: e.g., test everything everywhere. But this choice of activity isn't random, either.

One of our possibilities is to operate in a world of specifics. Therefore, to create this world, we need specific procedures to follow over and over. These repeatable steps produce feedback loops, and this feedback informs the changes to make to the software (code and defects), features, non-functional characteristics, and operational changes to reduce the support required. You must use the same process to generate the feedback loops so that each experiment (test) follows a similar process.

What does this mean?

Consider using a compass in the wild. You are out in some rocky wilderness—hills, rocks, plenty of trees, and your line of sight is never more than about thirty yards or so. You need to get back to your camp and know it's west of where you are right now since you hiked east by using your magnetic compass. The surroundings do not look familiar, but there is still plenty of daylight. So you are fairly sure you can navigate back.

Do you:

1. Navigate back using your compass.
2. Throw away the compass and use the sun.
3. Guess which way to walk and start walking quickly to get back before dark.

You use the compass. Why? The operating procedure to return to camp is to head west. And your tool of choice to find west is the compass.

Unfortunately, software and operational teams often wander around or change tools midstream without a real rationale.

If you leave with a compass, return with the compass.

Standard Operating Procedures

Imagine you are making spaghetti and meatballs for your family dinner. This sounds simple, and you've made it many times, and the family has eaten it up. How does this process go? Let's start with the sauce, and you proceed thus:

1. Heat olive oil on medium-low in large pot for sauce.
2. Chop onions, carrots, and celery.
3. Add vegetables to pot and let them slowly cook to create the base. (Vegetables sweeten when cooked low and slow).
4. After they are softened, at least twenty minutes, add whole peeled San Marzano tomatoes to pot, salt, pepper, increase heat to medium, and cover for one hour, stirring every fifteen minutes to prevent sticking and burning.

5. If the sauce starts to burn, reduce heat and add two tablespoons of water.
6. (Abbreviating now) Prepare, form the meatballs, and fry.
7. If cooking two pounds of meatballs, use two frying pans.
8. If stovetop is full, bake meatballs at 425 degrees for twenty-five minutes.
9. Cook the spaghetti in boiling water.
10. Serve.

This is a standard operating procedure. It outlines the procedures to follow to start work and provides guidance on the procedures to then follow when circumstances change—like in step 4 above. The goal of writing a standard operating procedure is to create consistency and safety.

Imagine if you didn't have a process to follow when making spaghetti and meatballs and you did it different every time. Putting raw meatballs in a cold pan or adding the raw onions to a completed pot of sauce isn't going to yield the results required. Letting the sauce burn makes it not so tasty anymore, which means it's not a usable product.

Of course, to create the maximum amount of chaos, make this meal without the instructions and bring in three other team members with their own opinions!

Standard operating procedures are like recipes with contingencies.

Long-Term Fixes and Mitigations

As the team triages and troubleshoots production incidents, they will find a few things:

- Reoccurring issues.
- Black-swan types of unpredictable issues.

- Unreproducible issues.

All of these need a mitigation plan.

What is mitigation?

Mit-i-ga-tion:

The action of reducing the severity, seriousness, or painfulness of something

Any problem you want to go away needs a mitigation strategy. That's it. Find out what it takes to make the problem not appear again, and you're set. Let's look at a few examples.

Example 1 - Reoccurring

Issue: The application is critically slow for the last two days of every month.

Root Cause: Users run end-of-month reports at the same time.

Mitigation: Add application caching for large reporting runs and two new reporting servers.

Example 2 - Unpredictable

Issue: Off-hour pricing updates on the warehouse are no longer finishing by 6 a.m. CT.

Root cause: The sales team sold one thousand new seat licenses to a large customer in an oppositive time zone. These one thousand new users are overwhelming the system during the hours of 1 to 6 a.m. CT.

Mitigation: (1) Move pricing calculations up by two hours and add twelve more vCPU's to the cluster to finish before this customer comes online. (2) Set up new communication channels with the sales team to prevent being caught off-guard.

Example 3 - Unreproducible

Issue: At 12:10 p.m. CT Monday, all fund prices showed "NaN" on the Reporting App. By 12:15 p.m. CT, all prices were back to normal.

Root cause: Unknown

Mitigation: Unknown. Research continues.

The sum of mitigations is to fix issues before they become major problems by organizing action lists and executing them back in your plan evolutions.

OPERATE

Flatten the Ops Curve

> *Danger, Will Robinson.*
>
> The Robot, *Lost in Space*

We can measure system complexity through effort, number of components, or dollars spent. All three of these can meaningfully represent the concept of system complexity. We will measure this on the y-axis in figure 9.6 below. The x-axis represents time.

The danger comes when the rate of operational complexity of a system scales linearly with the development complexity of the same system. This relationship doesn't need to be inverse, since that would be impossible in modern systems, but it should not scale at the same pace. See figure 9.6 below.

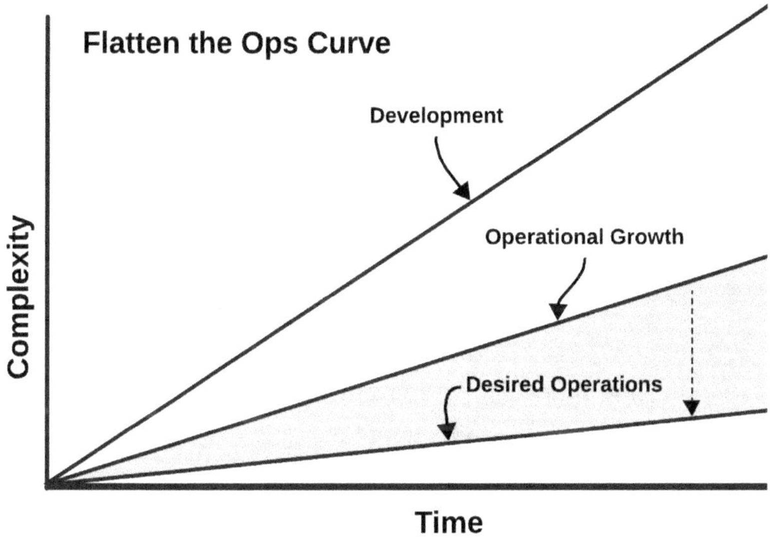

Figure 9.6. Flatten the Ops curve

The black line (1) shows the complexity of the development effort over time. It will go up. You cannot stop this—any system where code and functionality are actively added or changed will have its overall complexity increase. Don't even try to bend this rule—it's like gravity.

Code is complex, and it grows. Why? Think about writing the algorithms for an investment application. These algorithms are created in code to reflect a mathematical methodology and set of calculations created by experts—the domain complex. Now, let's say we have to model a one-year horizon and then a two-year horizon next month. Not a big deal, right? Ok, now model a three-year investment horizon, including variables like income at retirement, retirement age, spousal income, number of dependents, and held-away assets. Yes, now we are playing with fire, and this code will be full of conditional statements, which is where software complexity originates. "If this, then that" is a powerful construct that holds the power of success or failure on every CPU clock cycle.

Summary

The patterns of software construction in this chapter and the last are simple, but not easy to implement. Therefore, the entire set of patterns are rolled into a progressive, step-by-step system. Software systems aren't snowflakes. There is so much that's the same, repeatedly. It's why there is so much burnout in this industry while we want to pretend it's new. When we acknowledge what we do is a systematic, repeatable process—everything becomes easier.

Newton didn't invent gravity. We aren't inventing quality. It's already there—you now have a new way to think about it.

Patterns are good. Processes are great. But now, we see systems are the best—because they pull everything together.

Conclusion

The Boeing 737 Max challenges eventually turned around. Boeing dug their way out of their messes with federal officials, the legal system, and quality control. By dramatically changing their practices so that quality was captured at each stage of manufacturing, Boeing may still have a positive ending as Boeing increases production of the jet.

Much like Boeing's transformation, the journey to sustaining quality in software development hinges on the willingness to confront hard truths and adjust practices at every step. By embedding quality checkpoints throughout the process rather than relegating them to the final stages, organizations can avoid crisis-driven fixes and instead foster a culture where excellence is expected, not exceptional. This proactive approach empowers teams to anticipate issues, adapt efficiently, and deliver solutions that stand the test of time, underscoring the profound impact of systematic change on long-term success.

Throughout this book, you've read about techniques, viewpoints, and equivalencies within the low-cost, high-quality paradigm. In part 1 of the book, we looked at some raw truths, starting with: Most is barely okay. It's poorly built, poorly tested, and without any documentation or familiarity of purpose, let alone intentional design. Bolt on mounting cybercrime problems and the disagreement of what quality even is, teams and companies are perpetually set up for failure. Then we were forced to witness that the stalwart of defects (bugs) lists was mainly useless, accepting that an absence of defects says nothing about quality.

Teams must make nonstop decisions, sometimes democratically, sometimes through traditional management chains, but most often out in the field, on "the highways and byways" of project work—informally. Significant decisions are often as cavalier as deciding on what to have for lunch. Unfortunately, the decision between a sandwich on white or wheat doesn't yield the same impact. The right choice is to slow down. Reduce speed to reduce churn. Reducing churn has a positive correlation to raising quality.

Software outside of the major technological advancement of humanity or industry focuses on reducing cost. Software that is hard to change is expensive, but software which is expensive to purchase may not be hard to change. The correlations, though bidirectional, may not move in the same direction.

In part 2, we explored how assigning the right project design to your endeavor has such a high degree of impact on delivering quality. By managing risk and avoiding re-work, churn goes down and quality comes out. It's a prime, real example of low-cost quality by pulling levers that have nothing to do with the code of the solution. Much like the right contractor for a kitchen redesign is critical, so it is the same here.

And finally, and just as consequential as anything else in the book, using a software construction system like LIFT to increase consistency, eliminate confusion, and bake in quality practices from beginning to end makes life easier for everyone.

Godspeed and good luck with all your software journeys.

Acknowledgements

The business of software is what it is because of all the smart, curious and amazing people. I want to thank everyone involved in the construction of software systems and projects—you make this world work! To everyone I've had the opportunity to be led by, to observe or to lead—thank you for being you.

The experiences early in my career, like many leaders later, were inspirational and transforming. Managers like Diana from early on probably don't even remember me anymore! Krams and Dave—thanks for teaching me about patience. Thank you to folks like Vivek and Greg at Morningstar for their leadership example and giving me a chance. Thank you to James McClamroch for believing in me when I did not and being an excellent mentor. Thank you to Perry Marchant, who is one of the greatest technologists I've ever known and an excellent mentor for his listening, caring and providing feedback during the writing process. Perry taught me that if it's not in C++, it's probably not right!

Our team at DFIN is amazing! Thank you to impressive leaders and peers like Josh Duncan, an outstanding product management executive and everything he teaches me on a regular basis. Thank you to Chris Benes—you are an outstanding individual, and your professionalism makes everyone around you better daily. Thank you to the upstanding and outstanding executive team who seamlessly balance shareholders, employees, and customers.

Most of all, thanks to Floyd Strimling, our CPTO at DFIN. Floyd—this iconoclastic, amazing leader took a chance on me and has been utterly supportive to me as a professional, my career and more importantly to me as a human and my family. Words will never by enough—thank you.

I also want to thank industry thought leaders who inspired me—even though they don't know me. Thank you, Kent Beck, Martin Fowler, Gerald Weinberg, Kathy Sierra, Eric Freeman, Gene Kim, Rebecca Wirfs Brock, Bob Martin, Michael Feathers, Neal Ford, Nassim Nicholas Taleb, Michael Lewis and Jocko Willinck.

Thank you to the fantastic team at Gatekeeper Press for their professionalism, talent and patience during the writing, editing, design, and assembly of this book.

Soli Deo gloria

Appendix

Halfway through the writing of this manuscript I discovered a book from the 1970s with the same title: *Quality Is Free*. This book is not related to that book in any shape or form.

Topic Index

A

B

C

D

M

N

O

P

Q

R

S

T

U

V

www.ingramcontent.com/pod-product-compliance
Lightning Source LLC
LaVergne TN
LVHW022209200926
848481LV00006B/1908
9781662970450